NEW - from The RDA Publishing Group
The *ONE* book every retailer should own...

WINNNG IN RETAILING

SUCCESS

STRATEGIES THAT WILL:

- *Increase Your Store's Sales!*
- *Increase Your Store's Profits!*
- *Enhance Your Store's Image!*

D0841287

By James A. Rasmus and Gerald D. Rasmus

WINNING IN RETAILING
Success Strategies that will:
Increase Your Store's Sales! – Increase Your Store's Profits! – Enhance Your Store's Image!

By:
James A. Rasmus and Gerald D. Rasmus

Published by:
RDA Publishing Group
P.O. Box 102 • Carlisle, PA 17013

Library of Congress Cataloging in Publication Data

Rasmus, Gerald D.
  Winning in retailing: (success strategies that will increase your store's sales, increase your store's profits, and enhance your store's image) / Gerald D. Rasmus, James A. Rasmus.
    p. cm. --(Winning in retailing)
    ISBN 0-9642781-0-3

    1. Retail trade--Management.   I. Rasmus, James A. II Title
  HF5429.R37 1994   658.8'7
                                     QBI94-1730

Library of Congress Catalog Card Number: 94-68263
Printed in the United States.

TABLE OF CONTENTS:

BOUT THE AUTHORS

James A. Rasmus

 Jim Rasmus is no novice when it comes to the retail industry. He has over 25 years of retail management and professional store design experience. Following graduation from West Perry Senior High School in 1965, near Harrisburg, Pennsylvania, Jim served four years in the United States Air Force including a tour of duty in Viet Nam. While stationed at Nellis Air Force Base in Las Vegas, Nevada, Jim enrolled at the University of Nevada, Las Vegas and earned his Bachelor of Arts degree in Art. Following graduation and completion of his military service Jim accepted a retail store manager position with Montgomery Wards. He gained valuable experience in all areas of retail store management including employee supervision, budgeting, planning and organization, and merchandising. In 1980 Jim accepted a position with Creative Retailing, Inc. as Vice President and Partner. In 1983 Creative Retailing relocated to Los Angeles. Jim was responsible for the store design, layout and space planning functions. Jim left Creative Retailing in 1988 and founded Retail Design Associates in Fremont, California. RDA provides professional store layout, planning, and design services to a growing list of retail clients throughout the United States.

In addition to providing comprehensive store design and consulting services to the retail market, Jim is a featured speaker at numerous retail industry trade shows throughout the United States and Canada. He has authored many articles on store design and merchandising for the pet store industry, the motorcycle and bicycle industry, the auto industry, and the book store industry. Jim has designed over 1200 stores throughout the United States during his career. He and his wife Patty reside in Fremont, California.

Gerald D. Rasmus

 Jerry has served as founder and President of the Rasmus Financial Group since 1981 and as President of RDA Publishing Group. Located in Carlisle, Pennsylvania, the Rasmus Financial Group provides comprehensive financial planning services to owners of small to medium size businesses. The services include retirement planning, insurance planning, tax and estate planning, employee benefits, and investments. The RDA Publishing Group specializes in producing and publishing books for the retailing and small business industries. A 1964 graduate of Blain Union High School, Blain, Pennsylvania, Jerry earned a Bachelor of Business Administration degree from Elizabethtown College with a major in Management and a double minor in accounting and marketing. In 1980 Jerry earned his Master of Divinity Degree (Magna Cum Laude) from Evangelical School of Theology, Myerstown, Pennsylvania. Prior to founding the Rasmus Financial Group, Jerry served as Dean of Students for a large business college in Central Pennsylvania.

Jerry has extensive experience as a seminar leader and speaker. He has conducted numerous seminars and workshops on financial planning and money management related topics. He was founding publisher and editor of "The Family Today / Christian Perspectives For Family Living," a quarterly family journal, and "The Central Pennsylvania Runner," a monthly running and fitness newspaper. Jerry is an avid runner competing on the Masters Track and Field circuit in the 400 and 800 meter events. He and his wife, Nancy, reside in Landisburg, Pennsylvania. They have a daughter, three sons, and one grandson.

In 1992 Jim and Jerry decided to work together to produce and publish a series of articles, reports and a newsletter focusing on the retail store industry. The objective was simple: to help retail store owners increase sales and profits. The Rasmus brothers have brought together over 40 years of financial, managerial, and store design experience to produce *WINNING IN RETAILING*, the first in an exclusive series of books dedicated to helping retail store owners and managers sell more and earn more. Future volumes in the *Winning in Retailing* series will continue to draw from their wealth of practical experiences to help every retail store owner or manager become more successful and profitable.

EDICATION:

This book is dedicated to all those individuals who make up the retail industry. Your efforts help bring together the goods and services produced with those who need those goods and services in one of the great and growing segments of our nation's economy —retailing.

We hope the information contained in this book will help you do your job even more efficiently, effectively and profitably. Our greatest desire is to help you increase your sales, increase your profits, and enhance your image in the eyes of your customers.

We also dedicate this book to several people that mean a great deal to us personally. First, to our mother, Blanche M. Rasmus. Mom, thanks for all the sacrifices you've made for us. We love you a lot. To our wives, Nancy and Patty, for your enduring patience, faith, love, and encouragement. And finally, to our children, Jamie and Lisa, Dan, Steve and Tim for being a continuing source of joy, pride, and blessing.

CKNOWLEDGMENTS

We have not attempted to cite in the text all the authorities and sources consulted in the preparation of this book. The list would have included government agencies, libraries, business periodicals, and numerous individuals.

There are, however, a number of individuals who do deserve special recognition for their valuable contributions in the preparation of *Winning in Retailing*. They include:

— **Alamo Cycle Plex**. Robert and George Sistrunk, owners. San Antonio, Texas.
— **Back To Earth**. Arthur Trupp, owner. New City, New York.
— **Carousel For Children**. Mary Ann Garcia, owner. Stockton, California.
— **Cunningham Cycle World**. Mike Cunningham, owner. Fayetteville, North Carolina.
— **Cycle Sports of Salem**. Dave Colfax, owner. Salem, Oregon.
— **Franmara**. Frank Chiorazzi, Sr., owner. Salinas, California.
— **Malotts Honda Yamaha**. Wes Malott, owner. Manteca, California.
— **Monterey Bay Book Shop**. Jerry and Estelle Cimino, owners. Monterey, California.
— **Nybakke Vacuum Shop**. Dave Nybakke, owner. Bloomington, Illinois.
— **Party Plaza**. MBE, Corp., owner. San Dimas, California.
— **Pet Project**. Richard Manoogian, owner. Novato, California.
— **Premium Pet**. Tim Bum owner. San Jose, California.
— **Sportland Honda Yamaha**. Steve Karsten, owner. Bloomington, Illinois.

We sincerely thank all these clients, friends, and associates for their help and contributions.

Cover Design: Susan Hauschildt, Fry Graphic Services, Mechanicsburg, Pennsylvania.

I NTRODUCTION

Winning Strategies and Your Success

There can be no doubt that the retail store industry has experienced some rather difficult times during the past ten years. Those who own or manage retail stores have felt - in sometimes rather dramatic ways - the effects of a declining economy, reluctant consumer spending, buy-outs, bankruptcies, failures, restrictions and reductions in the amount of money available for expansion, increasing government regulation of small business, escalating taxes at all levels, and a growing lack of quality employees. For those who have survived, or for those who still feel the burning desire to start their own business and reach for the American dream, this book is for you.

This book has been written to serve as a guide, a reference, a "back-pocket" manual that will help you successfully start and operate a retail store. We understand that you will experience many roadblocks and obstacles on the road to achieving success. We have attempted to put together a practical, hands-on, nuts and bolts manual that will serve as your guide to defining and achieving success in the retail store industry. The book will focus on providing you with proven, winning strategies for achieving success in your business.

The word *strategy* refers to a conscious effort to develop a specific plan in order to accomplish a desired goal. *Winning* is synonymous with victory - to fight, to endure, to struggle, to strive for victory. *Winning* means to succeed in reaching a specific goal. This book will provide you with proven strategies designed to help you succeed in achieving one specific goal: Winning in retailing!! To become and remain successful!! To achieve victory!! But victory and success will not come easily. You will have to fight, to struggle, to endure; you will have to be ready to do those things that unsuccessful store owners and managers refuse to do - and to do them *every day*. This book, *Winning in Retailing*, can help you to achieve success and victory. We can provide some of the tools and resources necessary to be successful, but you will have to provide the most important qualities - commitment, perseverance, dedication, integrity, and a strong work ethic.

Part One of the book will focus on "Preparing For Success." This section will examine winning strategies necessary to develop and communicate a positive success attitude; the tools required to design and implement a realistic business success plan; and describe how to surround yourself with a personal business success team.

Part Two of the book, "Planning For Success," will examine some specific professional design and planning techniques that will enable you to transform your store into a "selling machine." Among the winning strategies included in this section are: how to complete a personal store walk-through and increase sales and profits almost immediately; merchandise techniques that will transform the look of your store; how to redesign your store to sell more products; traffic flow strategies that promote impulse buying; and how to create strong, lasting and positive first impressions throughout your store.

Part Three, "Managing For Success" will help you develop winning human relations strategies. We start with your employees, focusing on the hiring, training and retention of quality employees (your most important business asset). We then turn your attention to the importance of developing winning financial strategies to ensure the long-term success of your business. Finally, we examine the nature of personal leadership skills - how to manage with a strong sense of vision and purpose.

Winning in Retailing is meant to be a guide - a resource. It is not meant to replace your efforts, your creativity, or your ingenuity. Success never comes easily. It requires persistence, diligence, hard work and an unwavering commitment to achieving your goals. We have written *Winning in Retailing* in order to help you develop your game plan for success.

PART ONE

PREPARING YOUR STORE FOR SUCCESS

"Choose a job you love, and you will never have to work a day in your life."
—Confucius

CHAPTER 1

DEVELOP AND COMMUNICATE A POSITIVE SUCCESS ATTITUDE

"Do your work with your whole heart and you will succeed—there's so little competition."
—Elbert Hubbard

INTRODUCTION

First, let me explain what this chapter is *not*. This is not another treatise on achieving success through a positive mental attitude. Nor is it another attempt to try to impose on you the author's values or convictions. You can find dozens of books, booklets and magazines in bookstores everywhere that teach the importance of developing a mental attitude that is both positive and success oriented.

This chapter is included in our book for one reason: Because we feel that a common denominator of most successful retail stores is an owner that has a clearly defined vision of what his or her store is all about and an ability to communicate this vision to everyone connected with the store (including customers as well as employees). It is the objective of this chapter to provide you with a blueprint for communicating your "attitude for success" to both employees and customers. A winning and success attitude must begin with *you*.

> "Hold yourself responsible for a higher standard than anybody else expects of you."
> — *Henry Ward Beecher* —

Make no mistake about it - when it comes to the success of your store, no one has more at stake than you. As the owner, you took the risks to start the store. Perhaps you left a secure job and income to fulfill a life-long dream to be in business for yourself. You had a vision of the kind of store you wanted, the products you wanted to sell, where the store was going to be located; you took the initiative to secure the necessary money to get started; you were the guiding force behind the start-up of a business that would help you achieve your personal and financial goals.

You have the ultimate vested interest in the success of your store. It is critically important to realize that you are much more than just the "owner" of your store. You must be a leader, a motivator, a planner, an organizer. But above all, you must be the inspirational force that ensures the current and future success of your store. You'll have no more important role to play as a business owner. To fulfill that role you must possess - and communicate - an attitude that is first positive and then confident. Winning and success truly do begin with you. You must set the "success-tone" for your business. You cannot expect more from your staff and employees than you do from yourself. It is your attitude that must reflect all that is positive about you, about your store, and about your definition of success.

DEFINING A POSITIVE ATTITUDE FOR SUCCESS

Before you can light a fire in the hearts of your employees, it must first be burning brightly in your heart. You must assume the leadership role in displaying a positive attitude for success. Before we continue with this chapter I believe it's important to define just what a positive attitude really is. You've probably been told hundreds of times by dozens of self-help experts just how important it is to have a "positive attitude." But the important question is: how do you know if you have a positive attitude for success? Attitude has been defined in part by Webster's New World Dictionary as *"a manner of acting, feeling, or thinking that shows one's disposition."* Stop and think about that statement. Your attitude is on display for everyone to see and evaluate 24 hours a day. Your attitude is a reflection of your disposition. How would others who come in contact with you every day describe your disposition? Your attitude tells others something about your thoughts and your feelings. Your attitude, therefore, will have a direct affect on your actions - what you say and do in a given situation every day.

Positive has been defined in part by that same dictionary as *"confident, assured, affirmative, making a definite contribution, constructive...."* Therefore, let's put the two words together and describe a positive attitude. A positive attitude is the *inner disposition of a person that is generally characterized as confident, assured, affirmative, and constructive. Such a positive disposition is communicated to others through our thoughts, words, and actions and is on display at all times. A person with a positive attitude is one who makes a definite contribution to the situation at hand.* Does this describe the kind of person you are? Does it describe the kind of person you would like to be? If you are ready to see your sales and profits increase then I challenge you to become not just the owner or manager of your store, but to become a leader and a practitioner of *a positive attitude for success* with both employees and customers. Here are some additional thoughts on the importance of cultivating and communicating a positive attitude for success to your employees and customers.

CULTIVATE AND COMMUNICATE A POSITIVE ATTITUDE FOR SUCCESS

1. *A positive attitude for success is not inherited - it is a quality that must be developed and cultivated daily.* Every day will produce situations that will enable you to demonstrate your disposition (your Positive Attitude for Success). Plans will go wrong, employees will make mistakes, customers will create problems - something will happen that will give you an opportunity to demonstrate the inner qualities of your disposition (the real you). Will others hear in your voice or see in your actions responses to adversity that are positive, constructive and affirmative? Will you manifest to others a sincere desire to convert a negative situation into one that will have positive results? This positive response must be learned, practiced and cultivated every day. It will not be easy. You will need to make a personal commitment to converting every negative situation into an opportunity to further develop your Positive Attitude for Success.

2. *Demonstrate a positive attitude for success in every area of your business.* Opportunities for demonstrating a positive attitude for success will occur everyday and in many ways. First, you will have opportunities in your personal activities. Focus on using every personal set-back or problem as an opportunity to put into practice a positive response to a negative situation. Second, you will have opportunities to demonstrate a positive attitude for success when dealing with your employees. You must make a commitment to being a model or example to your staff and employees. They must see in you a person that takes seriously the goal of responding in a positive and affirming manner to problems and unexpected events. You must communicate to your employees and staff the same expectations for them as you do for yourself. They must know that a negative attitude or a negative response to a problem (or a customer) is not acceptable in your store. You must lead by example,

especially with your employees. Third, you will have opportunities for demonstrating a positive attitude for success when dealing with customers. As much as we would like it to be true, the customer is not always right. You know that and your employees know it. However, you must never be guilty of communicating that knowledge to your customers - even the truly obnoxious and rude ones. Treat them positively and with respect (yes, it will be hard . . .) but remember this: every good deed you perform toward another person will one day be returned to you in ways you cannot begin to imagine.

3. *Expect a Positive Attitude For Success When Hiring Every Employee.* The communication and cultivation process must begin when you recruit and hire each new employee. You must personally possess a positive attitude for success. The importance of possessing a positive attitude must then be communicated to every potential employee you interview. Never lose sight of the fact that every employee you hire will reflect in one way or another your standards and expectations. What's important to you will become important to them. If you are a practitioner of a positive attitude for success and have effectively communicated your expectations to each employee, then they will, over time, become examples to others (staff, managers, associates, and customers) of that same positive attitude they have observed in you. The formula for achieving a positive attitude for success is not difficult: Possess, practice, expect, communicate, reinforce, and reward.

Possess: Possess a positive attitude for success yourself.
Practice: Practice a positive attitude for success in all areas of your business.
Expect: Expect every employee to be a practitioner of a positive attitude for success.
Communicate: Communicate your expectations to all employees from the very beginning.
Reinforce: Reinforce your expectations continuously and consistently.
Reward: Reward proper behavior at all times (meaningful rewards reinforce the best).

Every employee and staff member must be important to you. Every position in your store must become an important one - first to you as the owner or manager and then communicated to every other employee. The secretarial position must be as important to you as the purchasing manager position. The custodian and clerk positions must become as important to you as the sales manager and store manager positions. You'll be amazed at how this kind of positive attitude for success will promote and increase employee morale and loyalty.

4. *Train For Success and Reward Those Who Practice It.* Every aspect of your training should reinforce your expectations concerning the importance and place of a positive attitude for success in your store. Never conduct a training program without taking some time to teach or illustrate the importance and value of a positive attitude for success. Perhaps an employee has received a thank you letter from a satisfied customer or a letter of commendation for superior service - whatever the specific situation, use it to reinforce your commitment to the value of possessing and practicing a positive attitude for success.

Use your training meetings to reward employees who have demonstrated proficiency in this area. Present to them some type of meaningful reward for superior effort: cash gift, gift certificate for lunch or dinner, self-help books that you feel are of particular value to your staff, a weekend get-away package; it doesn't have to be an expensive gift or reward as long as it is meaningful and it is presented in front of your staff. This will reinforce far more effectively to your staff just how important possessing and practicing a positive attitude for success really is than all the words you may speak in a month.

THE VALUE OF A POSITIVE ATTITUDE FOR SUCCESS

The subtitle of this book is "Success Strategies That Will Increase Your Store's Sales...Profits...and Image." How can the successful implementation of this "Success Strategy" help to increase your sales and profits? Let me summarize just a few.

1. A *Positive Attitude for Success* will become the anchor that steadies you through the rough seas of problems, adversity, and disappointments in the day-to-day operation of your store; you will persevere where others might quit, thus increasing your chances for future successes (and more sales and profits).

2. A *Positive Attitude for Success* is contagious and will be practiced by those around you, employees and customers, making your store the best possible place in which to work and shop.

3. A *Positive Attitude for Success* will help you develop and maintain a loyal and dedicated customer following - resulting in growing sales and growing profits for your store.

4. A *Positive Attitude for Success* will result in increased employee loyalty and decreased turnover. This means lower hiring and training expenses, thus increasing your profits.

5. A *Positive Attitude for Success* will result in more customer referrals, thus increasing your store's sales and profits.

6. A *Positive Attitude for Success* will result in increased customer good will thus giving your customers added reasons to come back and buy from you - and not your competitors. The result: increased market share along with growing sales and profits.

7. A *Positive Attitude for Success* will keep you (and your employees) healthier (and happier), thus lowering your medical expenses - and increasing your profits.

8. A *Positive Attitude for Success* will help create an environment in which shoppers will want to stay longer in your store - thus increasing your opportunity to sell them more products, which will result in increased sales and profits.

Begin today to develop, cultivate and reward a *positive attitude for success* in your store. It must start with you - the owner/manager. You must expect this attitude from every employee and staff member. It must be sincerely rewarded at every opportunity. Procrastination in implementing this success strategy can be very costly to your bottom line. Don't wait another day to begin developing and cultivating a positive attitude for success *(You can't afford to be without it)!*

CHAPTER 2

DESIGN AND IMPLEMENT A REALISTIC BUSINESS SUCCESS PLAN

"Your chances of success are directly proportional to the degree of pleasure you derive from what you do. If you are in a job you hate, face the fact squarely—and get out."
—Michael Korda

INTRODUCTION

Did you ever wonder why some businesses succeed and some fail? Some businesses seem destined for instant success (great concept, great product, great location, great timing, etc.), only to end up on the growing scrap heap of failed businesses, usually within 12 months of opening their doors. Other businesses with much less going for them seem to not only survive, but they grow and prosper and become huge financial successes. Why? One of the key answers to this question is usually found buried beneath the surface of most business start-ups. Businesses that survive and thrive seem to have a common denominator: the owners are firm believers in and practitioners of Business Success Planning.

Businesses that fail seem to also have a common denominator: the owners are firm believers in and practitioners of "seat-of-the-pants" business planning. They plan only when forced to, and even then they do it reluctantly, if at all. The old cliche is absolutely true: "People (or businesses) don't plan to fail, they fail to plan." The point is obvious. If you want to increase your chances of surviving and succeeding in your business, then develop and implement a Business Success Plan. This chapter will give you the tools necessary to do this.

The chapter will focus on the following: (1) Success Must Be Planned; (2) Business Success Planning Benefits; (3) Developing Your Business Success Plan; (4) Implementing Your Business Success Plan; (5) Reviewing and Adjusting Your Business Success Plan.

SUCCESS MUST BE PLANNED

I remember very well the first time I had to drive from my office in central Pennsylvania to meet with the Chaplain of the United States Senate in Washington, D.C. I was not looking forward to this drive. First of all, I hate driving with a passion, even on roads I'm familiar with. Second, I was being told all kinds of horrible and frightening stories about driving on the streets of DC and how easy it was to get lost and how dangerous the drivers were; I was developing a real paranoia about this trip. I decided that the best thing I could do was to plan this trip right down to the last detail to make sure I arrived at my destination on time and without incident. So I went to our local travel office and had a trip itiner-

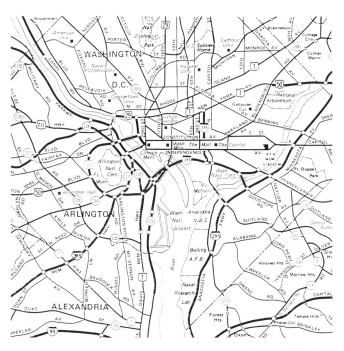

A good roadmap makes travel much easier. So, too, does a well thought out business success plan make your job of achieving a winning retail store much easier.

ary prepared with each road to be taken clearly marked, each street to be taken in Washington highlighted, alternate routes listed in case of construction delays, and telephone numbers of key people to call in the event of an emergency. Well, I'm happy to report that everything went pretty much as planned and I arrived safely and on time for my appointment. I would hate to think what might have happened had I not taken the time to adequately prepare and plan for the trip (I'd probably still be driving the streets of DC trying to find my way back to Pennsylvania . . .).

And yet thousands of individuals every year embark on a journey much more complex, incredibly more risky, and far more dangerous than my trip to Washington: they start or attempt to start a business *without any preparation or planning whatsoever!* Is it any wonder that almost eight out of every ten business start-ups each year end in failure? Did all of these individuals start out planning to fail? Probably not, but that's what ended up happening. Why? Because they chose to embark on one of the most important journeys of their life without adequate preparation and planning. They had no roadmap to guide them; no sense of direction or purpose to sustain them in times of adversity; and no real knowledge of where they wanted to go. They courted failure - and experienced it. By not planning for success, they planned for failure.

Perhaps you've been in business for some time. Or you may have just opened your store recently. Or you may be considering venturing out on your own for the first time to start a business. Whatever your current status, it is imperative that you stop what you're doing, read this chapter, and begin today to develop and implement your Business Success Plan. Make no mistake about it: Success must be planned - it doesn't just mysteriously happen without conscious effort and lots of hard work.

BENEFITS OF BUSINESS SUCCESS PLANNING

To make the planning process a little more palatable it is often beneficial to look at the end result of making the effort. Let's examine some of the benefits you'll experience if you take the time to develop and implement your Business Success Plan. Successful business planning will:

1. *Produce a sense of direction and purpose for you and your business.* You will possess a confidence that comes from knowing why you're in business, what your mission is, where you are going as a business, and how you will get there. You will wake up each day and know not only where you are headed as a business, but how you intend to get there. You will be prepared for dealing with problems, adversities, or unexpected events that most assuredly will occur. A strategic business plan becomes your personal "roadmap" guiding you each step of the way on your journey to success, sales and profits.

2. *Help you focus on the big picture.* As a store owner and businessperson you will too often become involved in putting out the many fires that arise on a daily basis. When that happens it becomes very easy to lose sight of the "big picture." You grow so accustomed to seeing the individual trees that you fail to see the forest. Strategic business planning forces you to keep focused on the big picture - especially in times of crisis and adversity.

3. *Enable you to sleep a little sounder at night.* Just knowing that you have a Business Success Plan in place and are successfully using it to manage and grow your business creates a sense of peace, order

and well-being; all of which will help reduce anxiety and tension. You'll be able to enjoy the exhilaration that comes from running a well-organized and successful business enterprise.

4. *Provide you with a standard by which to measure your efforts.* Just think what it would be like to watch a professional baseball or basketball game if the teams didn't keep score. Yet, many store owners are in business and have no idea what the score is when it comes to their financial success or failure. A business plan helps you establish goals and objectives and provides the means by which you can measure your progress in accomplishing those goals.

5. *Help keep you engaged, informed and excited.* Implementing a strategic Business Success Plan will force you to be involved in the overall operation and direction of your store. You'll be an active player on a day-by-day basis in the unfolding drama that attends managing and growing your own business. In addition, successful business planning will provide you with the tools and resources necessary to remain informed and knowledgeable regarding every aspect of your business. No longer will events determine direction and results - *you* will be in control. You will shape the events that are important to you, your employees, your customers, and your store. Finally, implementing a Business Success Plan will restore a sense of excitement about running your business. There will be a renewed feeling of enthusiasm and passion about your store and its success.

DEVELOPING YOUR BUSINESS SUCCESS PLAN

Are the potential benefits you can experience from developing and implementing a Business Success Plan worth the time and effort? Absolutely. The next step on the road to experiencing those potential benefits is to develop the actual business plan. It should be noted that there are many excellent books available to you on the subject of developing a detailed business plan. The purpose of this chapter is serve as an introductory guide for you in the development of a business plan. We would encourage you to go to the library and see first hand the wide range of books available on this subject. They will vary from the basic to the complex; from short easy-to-read treatises to the very complex and detailed text book treatment. You'll find something to suit your level and depth of planning desired. This section will examine in an introductory manner the basic components of a Business Success Plan.

Putting a business success plan together is going to take time. As a store owner/manager, it is important that you set ample time aside to begin the process of preparing your Business Success Plan. You should select a quiet location away from the activities and distractions of your store. You should request that you not be disturbed if at all possible. You should also expect to invest about 3-4 hours in this first session. You will need to bring to the location the following items and materials:

—Pen, pencils, legal tablet.
—Copies of your personal and business financial records for the past two years including - budgets, tax returns, net worth statements, bank account statements, investments, income and expense ledgers, sales reports and projections (if you have such documents).
—Be as well rested as possible.
—Be patient and persevere in your efforts.

Components of your Business Success Plan should include, but not be limited to, the following items:

1. *A statement of philosophy or mission.* Write out the reason or reasons you want to be in business for yourself. Why this particular type of store? How do you plan to be different from your competitors? What products or services do you want to offer the public and why? Essentially, you are asking and answering the question: Why do I want to own and operate this particular business? Focus on those qualities or attributes that will set you apart from your competition in the eyes of your customers.

2. *Defining your market.* To whom will you market your products or services? Why this particular market? Have you done any market research that would lead you to believe you will be successful in marketing to this customer group? Can this market comfortably afford to purchase your products or services? Is the market sufficiently large enough to provide the income you need to be successful? Can you possibly market to other groups? Which ones?

3. *Defining your competition.* Who is your competition? Are there competitors already in your market area? Are they financially profitable and successful? How many new business start-ups have there been in your field (and geographical area) during the last 12 months? 24 months? How many of them have survived more than one year? Can your market accommodate another competitor? Is yours a buyer's or seller's market? If there are other competitors, how will you separate yourself from them? What will you do differently than they do to attract and keep customers?

4. *Establish detailed personal and business goals.* If your business is successful, how will you know it? What is your definition of "successful?" What goals would you like to achieve for yourself? Your family? Your business? What timetable have you established to accomplish those goals? Are your goals predetermined, realistic, attainable, specific, and measurable?

5. *Establish a realistic personal and business financial plan.* This is a critical element in the preparation of your Business Success Plan. You must clearly define what income your business will have to generate in order to provide for both your personal and family financial needs as well as your business expense needs. It will be necessary to sit down with your spouse (if applicable) and prepare your family budget (income and expense needs). Next, do the same thing for your business. The total of your personal and business budget needs will determine the volume of sales required from your store operation to meet your financial obligations.

6. *Develop a specific advertising and publicity/promotion plan for your store.* Nothing will frustrate you more than to know you have a quality business in a good location, offering quality products or services at competitive prices, providing superior customer service, and still not experience sales success. One of the most frequent reasons cited by customers for not shopping at a particular store is this: "I didn't know they existed." Your Business Success Plan will be incomplete unless you include a comprehensive plan to promote and publicize your store. There are many excellent books written on the subject and we suggest another trip to your library to find one that meets your needs. You should, however, be aware of the differences between advertising and promotion and publicity.

Advertising refers to activities you will generally pay for in order to get your store's name in front of the public. Successful advertising efforts will necessitate that you determine what you want the buying public to know about your store and its products or services. Options available might include: (1) newspaper advertising, (2) radio and TV advertising, (3) direct mail advertising, (4) coupon advertising, (5) billboard advertising; (6) specialty advertising products (pens, pencils, calendars, etc.); (7) supporting community events or youth sports teams.

Publicity refers to those opportunities you may have to inform the buying public about your store without having to pay to do it. Examples include: (1) news releases on current topics or events; (2) community involvement activities; (3) new employee hires or promotion announcements; (4) charitable organization support, etc.

Your Business Success Plan should include the development of a strategy to continuously keep the name of your store in front of the buying public on a favorable basis. Use both publicity/promotion activities and advertising opportunities to the degree that your budget will permit. The important thing to remember is that this task needs to be included in your plan and in your budget.

7. *Design, develop and implement the use of an Employee Handbook.* Careful attention must be paid to the needs of your employees. They are your most valuable asset. They will become a reflection of what you determine is important in the operation of your store. Employees must be recruited and hired with this fact in mind. You must establish standards and expectations for all employees. Recruit and hire up to those standards; never lower your standards simply to fill a position with a warm body. An important tool available to you to help communicate your standards, rules, guidelines, and expectations is the Employee Handbook.

The Employee Handbook should contain all the information an employee needs to know in order to function as a valuable, contributing member of your store's team. Among the items that should be included in the Employee Handbook are: store philosophy and mission, history of store and founder, market served, employment policies, company benefits, compensation arrangements, rules and regulations. This document should be developed while your business is still small and manageable. However, even if you have been in existence for some time and still have not developed an Employee Handbook, you should do so as quickly as possible.

IMPLEMENTING YOUR BUSINESS SUCCESS PLAN

Once you have taken the necessary time to develop and write out your Business Success Plan, you're ready to tackle the hardest task - implementing the plan. One of the most frequently given reasons for not implementing a strategic business plan is that the store owner now feels he must "live up" to its standards and expectations. This can be a very intimidating and frightening prospect. It means that you - as the owner - must exercise self-discipline in the daily operation of your business. It means that you will be the one ultimately accountable for your business success - or failure. And this truth - that you are the one ultimately responsible and accountable - should be the single strongest motivation for taking this important step and implementing your business plan.

1. *Discuss and review the completed plan with your business associates or your spouse.* Seek out someone you trust and someone whose counsel you value to review the document with. This person should be someone that will speak honestly and candidly with you. Listen to their comments and suggestions. Accept what you feel is valuable counsel and make the necessary changes to your plan.
2. *Commit the entire plan to writing and make copies for review and analysis by your management team.* Review it with them. Encourage discussion, comments, suggestions, and recommendations. Again, sift through the suggestions offered, retain those that make sense, and make any necessary changes to the plan.
3. *Call a meeting with your employees and discuss the implementation of the plan with them.* Obviously, not everything in the Business Success Plan will be discussed with either your management team or your employees. Some of the information in your plan is very personal and confidential and should remain so. It is necessary, however, that you establish open lines of communication with your staff and employees. You should make a sincere effort to include your staff and employees in a discussion of your goals and objectives, especially as those goals and objectives relate to them.

REVIEW AND ADJUST YOUR BUSINESS SUCCESS PLAN
Every Business Success Plan must be periodically reviewed and adjusted. Initially, this review process may be as frequent as every quarter or six months. As the plan stabilizes, reviews may then occur on an annual basis. Reviews should be accomplished at least annually. Remember - for any plan to be successful it must be flexible.

You should not view the Business Success Plan as a document that will prevent you from responding to unanticipated events or occurrences as they affect your store or business. This is your plan and should reflect your values and convictions. It should be reviewed and adjusted as frequently or infrequently as you feel is necessary. The Business Success Plan is simply a tool - a resource designed to help you enjoy your business and to make your business more successful and profitable.

BUSINESS SUCCESS PLAN:
SAMPLE DESIGN AND FORMAT
A well written Business Success Plan will be both detailed and comprehensive. This is especially true if you may be thinking about applying to the Small Business Administration or a lending institution for a start-up or business expansion loan. Summarized below are some suggestions for plan content and format. Evaluate each of the sections and determine what is appropriate for you and your particular business. Remember - any plan you develop must reflect your business, your goals, and your desires. You must define what success means to you, then develop a plan that will enable you to achieve that success.

PART 1: PURPOSE OR MISSION STATEMENT.
This will be your cover page. It should include the following information: name and address of your business; telephone and FAX numbers; your company logo (if applicable). On a separate page

continue with your mission or purpose statement. You will be answering the following questions in this section: Why do you want to be in business? What is the specific mission or purpose for starting your business? What will make your business unique?

PART 2: OVERVIEW OF YOUR BUSINESS.

This section will include a statement describing the nature of your business. What industry are you in? What are your products or services to be offered to the public? You should take plenty of time in thinking through this section.

PART 3: OFFICERS AND MANAGEMENT TEAM.

This section should include a description of your business management team. List the officers and managers and include a description of their background and experience. Make sure you emphasize their qualifications to manage your business. Include a discussion of how you will compensate your officers and management team. Also include a list of the professional advisors who will be working with you (attorney, accountant, financial advisors, banker, etc.).

PART 4: MARKET OVERVIEW.

Provide a description and analysis of your potential market. Who will buy your products and services? What strategies have you developed to penetrate this market? What is your anticipated share of this market? What are your opportunities for market expansion? Who are your principle competitors and how do you plan to compete with them? How will your products or services be priced? What are your marketing strategies? Describe the role of customer service in your business. How will you resolve customer problems and concerns?

PART 5: BUSINESS DEVELOPMENT.

How do you plan to organize your business? Where will your business be located? How accessible will it be to your customers? What are your strategies for building and expanding your business? What are your product sources?

PART 6: FINANCIAL INFORMATION.

This is one of the most critically important sections of your business plan. Make sure you do your homework here. Begin by developing comprehensive personal and business financial statements - include a personal net worth statement, personal budget, estimated business budget, sources of all start-up capital (list unincumbered cash available and borrowed cash). Also include in this section cash flow projections for one, two, and five year periods; profit projections for one, two, and five year periods; anticipated break-even point based on your projections.

PART 7: SUPPORTING DOCUMENTS OR SCHEDULES.

Include in this section any charts or diagrams ...job descriptions for your staff and employees ... sample forms or documents that are of particular importance to your business ... letters of recommendation that focus on your strengths and skills to make the business a success.

Be as thorough as possible in developing your business success plan. This is the document you will be using to convince others that your business can - and will - be successful. Your business plan will be presented to potential investors, loan officers, vendors, potential officers, managers, and employees - so make sure it is professionally prepared. A small investment of your time and effort here will pay huge dividends for the future success of your business.

CHAPTER 3

SURROUND YOURSELF WITH A BUSINESS SUCCESS TEAM

"You can't do it alone!"
—Bill Gore

INTRODUCTION

What is a Business Success Team? Before we answer that question, let's define the word "team." One dictionary has defined *team* in this way: "a group of people working together in a coordinated effort." A Business Success Team, therefore, is a group of people, selected by you, for the specific purpose of working together in a coordinated manner to make your business more successful and profitable.

Why is this important to you? Your Business Success Team is important to you for a number of reasons. First, the team will provide you with new ideas, options, and perspectives on

A Business Success Team can bring together the talents and skills of others to help you achieve success. Select each one with care, patience, and objectivity.

your business. As a store owner/entrepreneur you tend to see things from one point of view since you have the ultimate vested interest in your business. Your Business Success Team will broaden your perspective, offer differing points of view, and assist you in examining alternative approaches in dealing with issues affecting your business. Second, your Business Success Team will make available to you individuals possessing specialized skills and areas of expertise. They will serve as your team of "specialists" to help with planning, organizing, managing, and decision-making tasks. Third, your Business Success Team will be a source of counsel when you need someone to talk to about your business, about problems you may be experiencing, or about difficult decisions that you are facing. It always helps to have another shoulder to lean on when times get rough, or when you just need a trusted friend or advisor to talk to.

Keep in mind that the Business Success Team is supportive in function. The individuals you select to form the team should be people that complement your skills and abilities. They should be individuals you trust and individuals who will speak honestly and frankly with you at all times. Some will be on your team out of necessity; others because you simply choose to have them on the team. Regardless of the reason, the team you put together has one primary purpose: *to help make your business successful and profitable.* You are still the one in charge and control of your business; you are the one ultimately accountable for your success or failure.

BUILDING YOUR BUSINESS SUCCESS TEAM

The following section will highlight the prospective members who will make up your Business Success Team. You may add to this list other individuals we have not included. Not all of the potential team members we have listed may be right or appropriate for your store or business. Select those that are and make them part of your team. Whether you have been in business for some time, have recently started your business, or are just in the "considering" stage to start your business, the sooner you begin to put your team together the sooner you will realize the significant benefits available to you and to the future success of your store.

1. *Spouse.* It is vitally important that your spouse be part of your Business Success Team. Your spouse and family will be affected very directly by the success or failure of your business. The degree of involvement by your spouse should be discussed thoroughly. The role your spouse plays can range from that of an interested observer to a formal partner and decision maker. Choose the role that is right for you, your spouse, your business and, most especially, your marriage and family.

2. *Trusted friend(s).* It is essential that there be at least one person on your Business Success Team with whom you can talk openly, honestly and frankly. There may be occasions when you simply need to talk to someone about your business, problems, decisions that need to be made, or new ideas you may be considering. This person should be someone you know well and that knows you well.

The following potential team members possess business related skills necessary to the long-term success of your business and should be selected only after much careful consideration and deliberation by you. Above all, those you select must be individuals you trust and have confidence in to do what is right for you, your family, and your business.

3. *Attorney.* For obvious reasons your Business Success Team will need to include an attorney you trust. In addition, your attorney should be competent in business related matters. The areas your attorney will assist you with will include (but not necessarily be limited to) the following: drafting your will and estate plan, preparing your business documents (partnership agreements, incorporation set-up, buy-sell agreements, etc.), complying with all federal, state, and local building and employment requirements, and any other necessary matters that may be relevant to your particular business. Owning, operating and managing a store or business in today's society is a complex undertaking. We have become a society in which suing someone else for almost any reason imaginable is commonplace. Selecting a trusted, competent attorney for your Business Success Team should become one of your first objectives.

4. *Banking officials.* It is important when starting your store or business to establish a strong working relationship with a bank located near you. We recommend having your personal and business accounts with the same bank, if possible. Make an effort to personally meet the key people in the various departments you may have contact with: the loan department, customer service department, trust department. Establish a reputation for paying loans and notes on time or ahead of time. Establish a good credit reputation by taking out a small business loan and repaying it ahead of time (do this even if you do not need the money - borrow $1000 for six months and repay it in two). Your good reputation will precede you so that when you really do need the money, you'll have little difficulty in getting it. Also seek to establish a business line of credit. Make it a small amount to start, and establish a reputation for prompt repayment of amounts advanced. Then over time, increase the line of credit to a level you feel comfortable with. Become very familiar with your bank's fee schedule. Most banks today have established fees and charges for just about everything - don't be blindsided

when you get your first statement simply because you failed to do your homework. If your bank is not providing you with the level of service and support you desire, do not hesitate to let them know, preferably in writing. There are still some banks that have made a solid commitment to providing quality service and support to their business clients; if you are not satisfied with your bank and cannot resolve your concerns, seek out another one (and make sure your current bank officials know you are leaving, the specific reasons why, and which competitor you are choosing - no bank likes to lose good customers to a competitor).

5. *Insurance Agent/Financial Planner.* This individual will play an important role in helping you properly manage your financial affairs. It is important that you not neglect this part of your business. Proper financial planning now can keep you from making some very costly mistakes later. This member of your Business Success Team can help you coordinate the following: (1) making sure you have properly insured your business, products, building, etc.; (2) setting up and adequately funding your personal life, health, disability, liability insurance, and retirement plans; (3) setting up and adequately funding your business life and business disability insurance programs; (4) coordinating personal and business insurance plans to avoid duplication of coverages; (5) establishing an adequate employee benefit program; (6) ensuring compliance with federal requirements for personal and business retirement planning; (7) assisting you in establishing financial goals and objectives for you, your family, and your business; (8) providing you with investment options compatible with your goals, investment temperament, and investment objectives; (9) coordinating your financial plan with your will and estate planning needs; (10) assist in providing retirement planning options for you and your employees. As with the other members of your team, this individual (or firm) should be selected with care and objectivity. Work with someone who possesses the professionalism and experience necessary to do a good job for you, your family, and your business. Your local auto and homeowner agent may not possess the technical expertise necessary to properly handle the other, more sophisticated, areas of your financial plan. Do not hesitate to seek out someone who has the experience, skills, and competence necessary to do this job properly - it is your financial future that is at stake here. As much as possible, this person should be someone you feel comfortable with and is someone you absolutely trust. Do not be afraid to ask for a sample of the type of work the person or firm you are considering does. Do you know someone who has used the services of the individual or firm? Ask for a summary of how the individual (or firm) is compensated for their services. Are they compensated entirely on a commission basis? Fee only basis? Or a combination of both? Does the individual (or firm) represent just one company or several companies? Find out on what basis they recommend the companies they represent (many times company 'A' will pay the agent or representative a higher commission than company 'B' on an inferior product and the agent will sell that product, not because it is in the best interest of the client, but rather because he receives a larger commission . . .). Perform your due diligence when selecting this important member of your Business Success Team.

6. *Tax and accounting advisor.* As a store owner you will, as we have already noted, be called upon to wear many hats as your business grows and prospers. We strongly recommend that one of the hats you do *not* wear is that of accountant and tax advisor. Just as you would seek professional

representation in legal matters, so too should you seek out a trained professional to assist you with financial record keeping, tax planning and preparation. This is a highly technical and continuously changing arena; you will have neither the time, training, nor the technical competence to do an adequate job for yourself. Do not fall into another trap so common to business owners - letting a "friend" who "knows a lot about money" handle your financial and tax matters. Invest in a competent accountant and/or tax specialist as soon as you can afford to do so (can you really afford *not* to?) - it will be one of the smartest decisions you'll make. As with the other members of your team, select this individual with care and patience. Make sure this person is experienced in working with business owners such as yourself. When selecting this individual, make sure you discuss the following: academic and professional credentials, years of experience, client list, fees, services provided, any legal action that has been taken against them relating to the conduct of their business, continuing education courses they have they completed in the last year. Does the individual (or firm) come recommended by others you know? It is very important to seek out someone that possesses the experience, technical competence and professionalism necessary to do the right job for you and your business.

7. *Professional Store Planner/Designer.* One of the key members of your Business Success Team should be a professional store planner/designer. It is important to understand the role and responsibility of this person. A retail store planner/designer is a professional specializing in the design, merchandising, and fixturing of retail stores. The planner/designer can provide you with a complete and comprehensive package of services whether you are planning a minor remodel or a major store building or renovation program. As an example, Retail Design Associates provides our clients with the following range of services: personal walk-through evaluation and analysis of your store operation, recommending and procuring the right fixtures for your store and products, merchandising your store, space planning and utilization, store decor analysis and recommendations (including proper use of color, lighting, flooring, signage, etc.), and individualized consulting services. It is important to enlist the services of a professional store planner/designer as early in your planning process as possible. The planner/designer can help you coordinate the many elements of a store building or remodel program with your contractor, architect, etc. The planner/designer can become one of your most valuable resources throughout the remodel process providing you with options and choices that will help your store increase sales and profits.

8. *Architect.* If you plan to remodel or build a new store, you will want to engage the services of a registered, professional architect to handle those aspects of the planning and design process that are not provided for by your store planning and design specialist. If you are unfamiliar with architects in your area, perhaps you can ask your store planning/design specialist for referrals or recommendations. Do not make the mistake of thinking your architect can also handle the planning, layout and design of your store's interior. Unless they have specific retail store design and planning experience you will want to select someone else to handle this part of your project (see #7 above: Store Planning and Design Specialist).

9. *Merchandiser.* Once your store has been designed, built, and outfitted with the right fixtures, you may want to consider securing the services of an experienced store merchandiser to come in and provide training and guidance in utilizing the right merchandising techniques for your store and your product line. The proper merchandising of your store's product line can increase sales dramatically. Successful merchandising is an art that requires skill, experience, and creativity. Your store planner/designer may be able to recommend the services of an experienced merchandiser to you. Having this person come in to teach you and your sales staff proper merchandising techniques will be an investment that will return huge dividends to you in increased sales and profits.

10. *Real estate professional.* There may be a time when you will want to relocate your present store or purchase another one; or you may still be in the early stages of planning to open your first store. Whatever your status, if you are considering the purchase of land, property, or an existing store or business, we recommend you secure the services of a real estate professional who can assist you with the many details of such a transaction. This member of your Business Success Team will be able to do much of the "leg-work" in locating properties in the geographical location you desire and in your price range. In addition, this person can help you understand the many (and complex) financing options available and which are the best ones for you to consider.

CONCLUSION

This chapter has focused on the importance of building your personal Business Success Team. These are the individuals whose contributions can help make a positive difference in the operation of your store or business. Some of these members will be permanent members of your team; others will be selected and utilized only as needed. The important point to remember is this: putting this team together and utilizing their skills, experience, and counsel will help you achieve more sales, more profits, and more success.

PART TWO

DESIGNING YOUR STORE FOR SUCCESS

"Even if you're on the right track, you'll get run over if you just sit there."
—Will Rodgers

CHAPTER 4

SUCCESS BY DESIGN: WINNING STORES ARE PLANNED

"Successful retail stores have one thing in common: they were designed that way!"
—Author Unknown

INTRODUCTION

Did you ever wonder why it is that some retail stores are more successful than others? In many cases, they will sell the same products, be located in the same geographical area, and draw from the same customer base. Yet, one store will thrive and achieve success, while the other languishes and seems to struggle just to keep the doors open. Why? One answer is that successful stores didn't get that way by accident - they were planned. Long before the first product was placed on a shelf for sale a winning strategy was developed to ensure (as much as is humanly possible . . .) the success of the store. Every element of the store and its operation was planned and designed in advance in order to accomplish one goal: to stay in business and earn a profit. Contrary to the belief held by many retail store owners and managers, success is not achieved by luck or accident; success results when you bring together careful planning and professional design, quality products offered at a fair price, and a genuine commitment to customer service and satisfaction.

Your potential for success will be dramatically increased and enhanced if you know something about contemporary store planning and design techniques and strategies. This chapter will give you an overview of what some of those strategies and techniques are, and how they can be applied to your store. Our objectives are: (1) to help you create a positive buying environment for your customers; (2) to help you increase your sales and profits; and (3) to help you enhance the image of your store. *(See Photo 1:22)*

STORE DESIGN - WHAT IS IT?

Store design is a concept that has been around for a long time. When the caravans stopped by the cities of ancient Egypt, merchants and retailers probably realized that if they arranged their wares in a unique way, or if they arranged them in colorful manner, or if they perhaps raised them off the ground so they were more visible than the products of the vendor next door, they would sell more products. Those early merchants were practicing the concept of "planned success." A lot has evolved over the last two or three thousand years, but one thing has remained constant - successful retailers have always planned for their success.

Planning the design of your store means much more than buying a few fixtures upon which to display some products. We have summarized some of the important concepts and components that make up successful store design and planning. Our intent is not to make you a professional retail store planner; rather it is to make you aware of important design techniques that you might be able to apply to your store in order to increase your sales and profits, and without having to spend thousands of dollars to do so. A strong word of caution is in order at this point: do not, under any conditions, compromise on the quality of your store operation. If the techniques outlined in this chapter are beyond your capabilities, then we strongly recommend that you contact a professional store planner/designer as soon as possible. Too many owner/managers make the mistake of trying to do it all themselves in order to "save a few bucks" and end up making mistakes that cost many thousands of dollars more than in making the initial investment in securing the services of a design professional.

ELEMENTS OF SUCCESSFUL STORE DESIGN

1. *Location.* Is your store located in an area designed to maximize sales? Is it easy to get to by your customers? Can your store be easily seen by traffic? Is there ample and convenient parking available? Is your store located in a safe and well protected area? Does your location provide for expansion opportunities?

2. *Developing a Space Plan.* A space plan is a comprehensive analysis of the internal layout of your store. The space plan design will include recommendations for the placement of your products, fixtures, lighting, sales area, offices, warehouse and storage, customer service areas, registers and equipment. The goal of space planning is to maximize the use of all your store space in order to sell more products.

3. *Designing a Traffic Flow Pattern.* Are customers drawn to all areas of your store on purpose - by design and intent? Are they being given ample opportunities to engage in impulse buying on the way to or from the area of their primary purchase? Developing an effective traffic flow pattern will help promote the movement of customers from one area of your store to another - from areas of the store that receive the greatest exposure (entrances, elevators, escalators) to areas located in the rear or the more remote corners of the store.

4. *Store Fixture Selection.* Effective store design will focus on determining the right fixture for your products and merchandise. Using the right fixtures in your store will help increase sales, make your store look nicer, and provide a more customer-friendly shopping environment.

5. *Color Analysis.* Success in selling your products can be greatly enhanced through the effective use of color throughout the store. Color analysis will include a consideration of the following areas of your store: the walls, flooring, fixtures, product arrangement, lighting, signs, and employee dress.

6. *Product Merchandising.* A critical element in effective store design is the merchandising of your products. Merchandising refers to those techniques involved in promoting the sale of your store's merchandise, including the selection, pricing, displaying, and advertising of your products for sale. Effective design and planning will seek to maximize the merchandising of all products offered for sale in your store. The goal of a successful merchandising program is to increase impulse buying, thus increasing overall sales on a consistent basis for your store.

7. *Signage Considerations.* Successful store design will also focus on effective use of all signage, both exterior and interior. Professionally prepared signs and signage will attract more customers to your product lines and serve to increase your sales.

8. *Store Lighting.* Understanding what type and style of lighting to use with what products is a critical element in successful store design. Should you consider: Ambient lighting? Accent lighting? Task lighting? Track lighting? Direct or indirect lighting? Successful store planning and design will not overlook the importance of lighting as a source of increasing your product sales.

9. *Employees and Staff.* The most important asset in your store is not your products or merchandise. It is your staff and employees. Planning for success must involve thinking through your strategies for attracting, training, and retaining competent, knowledgeable, and customer-oriented employees.

DO IT YOURSELF OR USE A PROFESSIONAL?

The obvious answer is to use a professional store designer to help you if you have the resources available (i.e. money). It is well worth your investment of time and money to work with a retail store design specialist who can bring together all the interior and exterior elements unique to your store. A design specialist can prepare a comprehensive analysis of your store's current operation, provide you with specific recommendations in all of the areas mentioned above - recommendations designed to help you increase your sales, increase your profits, and enhance your image. Most professional planners can provide you with a wide range of choices in levels of service based on your budget and objectives.

You may also choose to implement a number of design strategies yourself. This book is written to help you do just that. It is very important, however, to be aware of the many components involved in a successful store design. Do those tasks you feel most comfortable and competent to do; do not hesitate to contact a professional retail store planner to help you with those tasks you have neither the time nor the experience to complete successfully yourself. Nothing less than the ultimate success of your store is at stake. *Remember, if you don't do it right the first time, it's twice as expensive the second time around!*

CHAPTER 5

COMPLETE A WALK-THROUGH AND INCREASE YOUR SALES

"I never dreamed that just walking through my store with open, objective eyes could be so revealing, so beneficial, or so potentially profitable!"
—Motorcycle Store Owner

SECTION ONE: WHY CONDUCT A STORE WALK-THROUGH?

A. HISTORY AND DEFINITION OF THE STORE WALK-THROUGH

I frequently have opportunities to conduct seminars at trade shows and expos throughout the United States. Following my presentations I am repeatedly asked by retail store owners and managers if there isn't something they could do - right now - to increase sales and profits without having to invest thousands of dollars in a major store remodel or redesign. Like many industries, retailing has experienced some tough economic times during the past few years and the outlook for the future appears to be mixed at best. In particular the small to medium sized independently owned retail store has been hit especially hard. Many owners and managers have not had the extra cash flow necessary to invest in a major store remodel or redesign, yet they have continued to express a growing need to do something to improve their bottom line. As a result, I have developed a unique program that addresses this need: the store walk-through and analysis.

The Store Walk-Through and Analysis was developed in order to provide retail store owners and managers with a comprehensive, systematic and organized approach to evaluating the overall operation of their store. At a mutually convenient time I would schedule an on-site visit to the store. During the visit (which generally lasts about a half to a full day) the owner would discuss with me the details of their entire store operation. I would then "walk-through" the entire store observing, evaluating and taking detailed notes. Included in the walk-through and analysis were the following components of the store and its operation: the store exterior, interior, traffic flow, product merchandising, fixtures, human resource procedures and policies including employee hiring, training, and development, customer shopping habits, customer service procedures, and store layout and design.

At the completion of the store walk-through a comprehensive, detailed, written analysis is prepared for the owner/manager outlining specific recommendations that could be implemented in order to improve and correct problems, enhance the store's image, and increase sales and profits. During the past ten years I have consulted with hundreds of retail store owners throughout the United States; as a result, I have discovered and compiled a number of ways retailers can improve their store operation and increase sales and profits.

B. THE BOTTOM LINE

I realize that it is not always possible for store owners and managers to hire an experienced professional retail design consultant to visit the store in person. I also realize that you nevertheless still desire to own and operate a growing, successful store. I strongly feel that if you are serious about achieving success, then you will need to make a commitment right now to studying and implementing the ideas and techniques revealed in this chapter. The results may be quite dramatic: an enhanced store image, a growing customer base, increased sales, more productive employees, and perhaps most importantly - a growing, more profitable bottom line for you and your store.

SECTION TWO: PREPARING FOR THE STORE WALK-THROUGH

A. GETTING READY

As with any worthwhile endeavor, success is the fruit first planted with the seeds of careful preparation. In order to achieve success with your store walk-through you will need to spend some time preparing. It might be a cliche, but it is nevertheless true, you'll get out of the walk-through what you put into it. Therefore, take some time to carefully review the recommendations that follow. This chapter will help you identify existing and potential problem areas in your store. In addition, this chapter will provide you with suggestions and recommendations that you can use to correct or improve problem areas, as well as provide you with ideas and techniques for preventing problems from arising in the future. Take time now to prepare. View this as an opportunity to invest in the future success and profitability of your store.

"Success is the fruit first planted with the seeds of careful preparation".

B. HOW TO PREPARE

After years of experience in conducting store walk-through's and consulting with hundreds of store owners and managers, I have determined that certain qualities and tools are required in order to complete a successful walk-through. They are summarized below.

1. *Be Objective.* The first, and perhaps the most important, quality necessary in preparing to conduct the store walk-through is to be objective. It won't be easy. As the owner or manager you are used to seeing your store everyday through eyes that have grown accustomed to the status quo. Much like a loving parent who looks at his son or daughter and sees only a lovely child without fault or imperfection (even when the opposite is true), so too do you, as owner of the store, see your "child" as being without fault or imperfection. I am now going to ask you to look at your store and see everything through objective eyes, or "customer eyes." Customer-eyes are unbiased eyes; eyes capable of seeing things as if for the first time; eyes capable of seeing not only that which is good, but that which may not be so good. You must put aside - as much as is humanly possible - any preconceived ideas and notions you hold about your store. You must strive to see your store operation as it really is. You must look at each component of your store operation with a critical eye. This is the "fresh set of eyes" approach that will be essential for your success in completing this project. To achieve the best possible results from the store walk-through you must be willing to set aside your personal feelings and become your own "professional consultant."

2. *Set Ample Time Aside.* This is a project worthy of your time and undivided attention. Therefore, I recommend that you plan in advance to set enough time aside to complete the walk-through without feeling rushed and with a minimum of distractions. I know you're busy. There are probably a hundred

things for you to do the moment you walk into your store. If you're going to profit from the material in this chapter, then you must decide to set aside enough time to do the job right. Depending on the size of your store and the number of units involved, I recommend at least 3 to 4 hours to complete the walk-through for store units under 5000 sq. ft. If you have multiple units, you may wish to do one unit at a time, spread out over several days. When is the best time to complete the walk-through? The best time is generally during off-peak sales hours. However, if possible, try to complete the walk-through during business hours so you have an opportunity to observe both customers and employees in the store. If you feel that conducting the walk-through is not possible during business hours then schedule it before you open, after you close, or on a day your store is normally closed. Again, the important point is this: set aside ample time to complete the walk-through.

3. *Tools Needed*. After you've scheduled an appropriate time to complete the walk-through and you've mentally prepared yourself to be as objective as possible, you will need to make sure you have the proper tools to begin. You'll need to have the following items at hand before you start the actual walk-through:

    (1) "Fresh set of eyes"
    (2) Clipboard, tablet, and pen
    (3) Tape measure
    (4) 35 mm Camera with several rolls of color film or Video Recorder or Camcorder

The clipboard should contain blank sheets of paper on which you can record comments and observations. In addition, you will want to record a brief description of the photos you take during the walk-through. The 35mm camera and color film (or the video recorder, if available) will be used to take pictures of the store as you complete the walk-through. You can't get any more objective than a photograph or film. The photos (or video) will be valuable if you decide to utilize the services of a professional store designer at a later date. The tape measure will be used to record dimensions of your store interior and exterior, the size of your sales areas, office and storage areas, etc. These measurements will be helpful in evaluating the effectiveness of your space utilization and may also be helpful if you decide to work with a professional store designer at a future date.

4. *Use An Assistant*. Using an assistant to help with the walk-through provides a number of advantages to you. First, the assistant can help with taking measurements, thus saving some valuable time. Second, an assistant can be designated as the official photographer, thus freeing you up to observe and record. Third, an assistant can also serve as another "fresh set of eyes" as you conduct the walk-through. Ask this person for their opinion and observations; does he see things as you do? An assistant can provide you with valuable feedback as well as give you a different perspective on what you observe during the walk-through. If you have employees, you may want to select someone recently hired to be your assistant. A recent hire will tend to be more unbiased in their observations (they simply have not had enough time to grow as used to things as you have). If you use a recent hire, make sure this person will feel free enough to speak the truth to you. Anything less than total honesty and objectivity will result in a waste of your valuable time and effort.

I realize conducting your own store walk-through and analysis will not be an easy task. You're going to be asked to come out of your personal "comfort zone" and to try to see your business in much the same way a potential customer would - through unfiltered, unbiased and objective eyes. Keep in mind that customers are not compelled to shop at your store (after all, there *are* other competitors...). They will shop at your store (or avoid your store) for a number of reasons. The purpose of completing a store walk-through is to determine if you are giving your potential customers compelling enough reasons to enter your store, to buy your products and to become a loyal customer. Doing your homework now could very well spell the difference between success and profits or failure and bankruptcy; of *becoming* the competition or *losing* to the competition.

SECTION 3: CONDUCTING THE STORE WALK-THROUGH

A. THE APPROACH
It's very important that the store walk-through be conducted in a manner that parallels the way a potential customer would approach your store for the first time. Most new customers will drive to your store, park the car, walk into your store and begin shopping. This is the same approach you should take in conducting your store walk-through. You should start outside, evaluating the exterior, make your way into the store, evaluate the interior, traffic flow, products, employees, and customers. Taking any store measurements can be done at the conclusion of the walk-through.

B. FIRST IMPRESSIONS (OR FATAL IMPRESSIONS?)
You've heard the old adage that "first impressions are lasting impressions." Well, it's true. You usually get only one opportunity to make a positive first impression. When meeting someone for the first time you immediately form an impression of that person the moment you see them - even before the first word is ever spoken. And that person forms an immediate impression of you. Your appearance, clothing, grooming, body language all come together to create an image - either positive, negative, sometimes neutral - but an image is nevertheless formed. And once that first impression is made it is very difficult to change the mind of the person forming the impression (this is especially true if the first impression formed is a negative one).

This tendency on the part of most of us to form first impressions applies to your store as well. You will usually get only one opportunity to create a positive first impression in the mind of a potential new customer. That potential customer may have seen your nice ad in the newspaper, or heard your catchy commercial on the radio, or received your enticing special offer in the mail, and now they are ready to go out of their way to visit your store. You've been successful in giving that potential customer a reason to come to your store, but have you done everything possible to make sure that every part of your store operation - from location, access, parking, the building, the interior, to the employees - will create a positive, lasting first impression in the mind of that shopper? Have you taken the time and made the effort to go that extra mile to separate your store from the competition (in a positive, rather than a negative, way)?

First impressions are so important that I will continually remind you of them throughout this chapter. As you evaluate the various components of your store operation you will be asked to write down your first impression - and to be as objective and honest as possible when doing so. First impressions are lasting impressions. Make sure the first impressions you create are positive impressions, not *fatal* impressions. The store walk-through and analysis will help you focus on creating a positive and customer-friendly first impression.

C. THE EXTERIOR

Your examination of the exterior should include the following: store location, parking areas, and building and grounds. *(See Photo 1.1)* It is important that you take some extra time and do the following things. First, gather up the store walk-through tools we described earlier in this chapter. Second, round up your assistant, get in your car, and approach the store on the same roads or streets most often used by potential customers coming to your store. If most customers walk to your store, then you do the same. If they take public transportation, then you do the same. It is important that you experience what your potential customers experience in trying to get to your store location. Only then will you be able to accurately evaluate your location and its impact on the success of your business.

1. *Your Location.* No other single factor is more important than location in determining the potential success of your retail store. I understand that many readers may not be able to do much about their store's location at this point. However, you should still take a good hard look at your present location. As I have already mentioned, it will greatly enhance the value of the walk-through if you take plenty of color photos of the appropriate items that are discussed below. Among the things to consider and evaluate are the following:

(a) Visibility - How visible is your store to the shopping public? Can your store be easily seen from a distance? Does your store stand out among the other stores near you? *(See Photo 1.2)*

(b) Convenience - Is your store conveniently located and easily accessible by customers? Can potential customers find your store with a minimum of hassle and trouble? Is it easily accessible by automobile, public transportation, walking? Convenience and accessibility are extremely important factors if your business depends on a high volume of walk-up traffic. *(See Photo 1.3)*

(c) Customer Profile - Do you rely on regular, loyal, repeat customers? If so, they will probably seek out your store regardless of convenience or accessibility. However, if your business relies on a continuous flow of new customers, impulse buyers or price-conscious shoppers, then a convenient, easily accessible location is critically important to you.

(d) Relocation Necessary? - After evaluating the type of customer you depend on for your sales, you may determine that relocating your store is a necessity. This is a major decision to make and will involve significant cost, time, and effort. The decision to relocate your store should not be made without first consulting with some experts. Contact a commercial real estate specialist to assist you in locating and evaluating possible new sites. In addition, you may want to contact a retail store design specialist to help you with the layout, design and merchandising of your new store. If you have the cash available, and can find the right location for your store, then a relocation may be your best alternative.

(e) Redesign or Relocate? - If relocation is not possible, you may wish to consider a partial or complete redesign of your existing store. This approach can breathe new life into your store's operation, enhance your image, create positive first impressions, and most importantly, boost your bottom line with increased sales and profits. Our recommendation is to contact a professional retail store design specialist to assist you with any remodel or redesign. This professional can provide you with a wide range of products and services to ensure that the remodel or redesign will be successful.

[*First Impression:* As you evaluate your store's location through the objective, unbiased eyes of a potential customer, what are your first impressions? Are they positive? Negative? Why? Record your impressions and those of your assistant as you continue with the store walk-through].

2. *Parking Area.* Unless you are in a mall or plaza location, customer parking is another important factor in determining the potential success of your store. You may have a great product, be in a good location, have an outstanding, dynamic advertising program, but still lose thousands of dollars in potential sales if you do not have an adequate parking area for your customers to use. When evaluating your parking area, you should consider the following factors (Remember: Take color photos (or a video) to supplement your written evaluation):

(a) Easily Accessible - How easy is it for customers to enter your parking area from the streets or roads surrounding your store? Do traffic patterns permit easy access to your lot? If not, can you do anything to improve the situation?

(b) Well Paved and In Good Repair - Is your lot well paved and in good repair? Do you make sure pot holes are repaired in a timely manner? If you are located in a cold weather area, do you keep the lot free of snow and ice during periods of inclement weather?

(c) Painted Lines - Does your lot have painted lines designating individual parking spaces? Are these lines painted on a regular basis and easily visible by your customers?

(d) Handicapped Spaces - Does your lot have an adequate number of clearly visible and well maintained handicapped parking spaces close to the main entrance to your store? Are there adequate walkways leading from the parking area to the store entrance for the handicapped? Do you have available a copy of the Americans With Disabilities Act guidelines and regulations? If not, contact the appropriate government office and have them send you a copy to ensure you are in compliance.

(e) Clean and Free of Debris - Is your parking area cleaned on a regular basis to ensure glass, nails and other debris is picked up and removed? Nothing discourages shoppers more than dirty, debris filled parking areas.

(f) Well Lighted - If your store has evening or night hours, is your parking area well lighted? Are burned out bulbs or lamp units replaced on a timely basis? Are the lights powerful enough to provide adequate lighting for all areas of your lot?

(g) Clearly Marked Entrance and Exit Signs - If your parking area has separate entrance and exit areas, are they clearly marked with easy to see and read signs? Are your entrance areas easily accessible from adjacent streets? Is on-coming traffic clearly visible as cars attempt to exit your lot? Is it easy (and SAFE) for exiting customers to enter the traffic flow as they leave your lot?

(h) Safety - Is your parking area safe? Can customers leave their cars and walk to your store in safety? Are customer cars safe while in your lot? This can be a very serious problem if your store is located in a downtown area or in a high crime area. If you are unable to relocate your store, then you must ensure some type of safety procedures are in place for your customers when they visit your store. Perhaps you may have to hire a security guard to patrol your lot, or enter into a cooperative arrangement with the local police department to provide extra patrols through your lot during business hours.

[*First Impressions*: What are your first impressions as you enter your parking area? Is it customer-friendly and does the parking area add to or detract from a customer's shopping experience when visiting your store? If there are some negatives associated with your parking area, list each of them on your worksheet and beside each negative write down any corrective action you plan take to remedy the situation.]

3. *Building and Grounds*. Our walk-through will now focus on your building and grounds. Again, if your store is located in a mall or plaza, this section may not apply and should be omitted from your walk-through and analysis. If applicable to your walk-through, I again recommend taking color photos of all appropriate areas for later review and evaluation.

(a) Sidewalks - Are there sidewalks or walkways leading to your store from surrounding streets or from your parking area? If so, are the walkways in good repair, clean, and safe? If you are responsible for sidewalk maintenance, do you clean and wash them down on a regular basis? If you are located in a cold weather area, do you ensure that snow and ice are removed on a timely basis and that anti-skid material is applied? Are weeds regularly pulled from the cracks during warm weather months?

(b) Landscaping - Do you have plants, shrubbery or trees on your property? Are they maintained on a regular basis to ensure they remain attractive and in good repair? If you have a lawn, is it mowed on a regular basis? Is trash, litter and debris picked up daily? Does the landscaping enhance your store's image?

(c) Store Exterior - Is the exterior of your store in good repair and is it pleasing to the eye? If necessary, is the building painted on a regular basis? Is care given to the selection of colors? Do the colors selected enhance the image of your store? Is the roof in good repair? Are windows, doors, shutters, and awnings in good repair and do they provide an attractive appearance as customers approach and enter your store?

(d) Windows - If windows are visible to the public, are they clean and in good repair (no broken panes or glass)? Are your windows free of all unnecessary signs and clutter that would give your store an unkept or a "busy" appearance? If you have window displays visible from the outside, are they neat, well organized, professionally prepared, and visually attractive to the eye? Are window displays changed or rotated on a regular basis? Are seasonal window displays taken down on a timely basis?

(e) Entrance and Exit Doors - Are all entrance doors to your store in good repair? Are they large enough for easy access, especially by the handicapped? Are they easily opened? Are they well lighted? Are they free of all unnecessary signs and clutter that would impede a safe, easy entrance and exit? Are exit doors from the store clearly marked for your customers?

(f) Signage - Take a good look at the main entrance to your store (in fact, make sure you take a couple of pictures). How visible are your store signs - especially from a distance? Can these signs be easily seen and read by passing traffic? Are your exterior signs clearly visible at night (do they serve as your "silent salesmen" during off-hours?)? Do your exterior signs accent and enhance your store's image? Are all exterior signs in good repair? Do they create a visually attractive and powerful image? Is the name of your store clearly visible? Are your exterior signs free of all obstructions and do they meet all local regulations and codes? *(See Photo 1.2)*

(g) Posted Hours - Are your store hours of operation clearly visible to customers? Is the sign displaying store hours professionally prepared (or is it hand-written)? Is the store hour sign well lighted for evening or night visibility? Does the sign enhance your store's image?

(h) Inviting Appearance - Is the actual entrance to your store inviting and customer friendly? Does it communicate a "welcome to our store" feeling to every customer? Do customers feel as if they are being "invited" to come in and shop, or do they feel intimidated or threatened? Do customers have to overcome physical or visual barriers to enter your store? Is the entrance to your store visually exciting, and does it create a sense of adventure as the customer enters your store?

[*First Impressions:* Do your building and grounds create a positive first impression? What areas can be improved? List them on your worksheet and indicate what specific steps you will take to make the necessary corrections or improvements.]

D. TRAFFIC FLOW

1. *Standing at the Threshold.* You should now be standing at the main entrance to your store. Before you begin your walk-through of the interior, stop where you are and take a look around the inside of your store. What do you see? Take a couple of pictures of the interior from this point. Does the store interior appear to be neat, well organized, clean, and full of products? Look around with a "fresh set of eyes" and consider your first impression of the inside of your store. Is it positive? Negative? Why? Write down your initial responses and impressions as you stand at the threshold of your store. Ask your assistant for his or her first impression. Now you're ready to proceed with the walk-through of the interior. Keep your camera ready to photograph each phase of the walk-through.

2. *Traffic Flow Defined.* Before you begin to walk through your store, stop for a moment at the entrance. As you stand there, determine in what direction you feel most comfortable walking. Are you naturally drawn to the right side of the store or the left side? Do you feel compelled to walk down the center of the store? Does the layout of your store dictate the direction the customer will take? If this is so, then you have experienced the concept of traffic flow. Traffic flow is a retail term that describes the predetermined direction customers will take when they enter your store. Remember, once you've

accomplished the objective of getting the customer into your store, the next objective becomes moving that customer through all (or as many as possible) of the departments of your store. You want to expose that customer to as much of your product line as possible in order to motivate them to make multiple purchases instead of a single (or no) purchase.

Traffic flow design is a technique that you can use to accomplish this objective. Consider your own store. Watch as customers enter your store. What direction do they take? Right - left - or center? Do most of your customers make a single purchase or multiple purchases? How much time do customers spend in your store? Are they in and out in a short period of time? Or do they tend to browse from

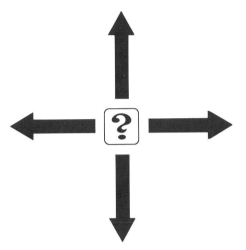

Are your customers confused? Do they know what direction to take when they enter your store?

product line to product line, picking up and examining multiple products? This is what you want to achieve and proper traffic flow design can ensure this type of customer response is repeated many times over.

3. *Traffic Flow By Design or Default?* Have you made a conscious effort in the design of your store to create a predetermined traffic flow pattern? If you have not, then you have created a traffic flow pattern by default. The customers will decide where in your store they will go and how they will get there. The customers retain strategic control - not you. The result: lost opportunities for additional impulse sales and, unfortunately, lost revenue. Consider the benefits to you on a long term basis (more sales, more profits) of developing a traffic flow strategy for your store. If unsure of what to do, or if you have specific questions about developing a traffic flow pattern for your store, we recommend that you consider contacting a retail store design specialist to discuss your situation in more detail.

4. *The Right-handed Phenomenon.* Studies have shown that about 80% of the population is right-handed and will, in most cases, move to the right when entering a store (unless, of course, they are prevented from doing so by physical or other barriers). This psychological predisposition is important to understand. Shoppers are for the most part creatures of habit. As a retailer, your goal is to create and reinforce shopping habits that will result in more sales - especially impulse sales. Shoppers will tend to move in a direction that feels most comfortable to them; a direction that is non-threatening and free of physical or psychological barriers. If moving to the right is a natural, comfortable response by the majority of shoppers, then create a store interior that makes it easy (in fact, encourages them) to move in that direction. You now have an opportunity to make sure the customer is directed to as many of the product areas in your store as possible.

5. *Floor Design Determines Traffic Flow.* *(See Photo 1.4)* Creative store designers recognized the potential importance of this right-handed phenomenon and proceeded to develop traffic flow patterns

that enabled retailers to take full advantage of this shopper response. One very successful technique developed was to utilize creative, predetermined floor design patterns to promote and encourage positive shopper habits. For example, the grocery store I shop in has one main entrance that all shoppers must use. However, once you enter the store, the floor design and pattern directs all shoppers to the right. Aisles and shelving units are arranged so that shoppers are moved easily to the right. Special carpeting is used that silently tells every shopper to "walk in this direction." The store now determines what products I will be exposed to as I make my way through the store. Most of the staples (milk, bread, eggs, meats) are located way in the back or on the left side of the store, making it necessary for me to walk the entire length or breadth of the store to get to these often purchased items. What happens en route? I'll see some soft drink, or chips, or cookies, or a deli item that I didn't really come in to purchase, but impulsively decide I "need" that item and since I'm going right by it I might as well throw it in the cart. Pretty clever, right? You bet. And it's all done on purpose using floor design techniques to determine traffic flow.

There are many types of flooring covers available that will enable you to implement a traffic flow pattern for your store. Prior to selecting a floor covering, you may want to evaluate the entire layout and design of your store's interior. The repositioning of merchandise, the use of modern store fixtures, applying creative merchandising techniques- all of these must be considered when developing a traffic flow strategy. Again, a professional store designer may be a tremendous resource for ideas and suggestions when considering changing the interior of your store. We'll cover traffic flow in more detail in Chapter 6.

6. *Merchandise Displays.* Another effective technique used to establish and direct customer traffic flow is the use of product or merchandise displays. You can consider placing the most popular or in-demand products in the farthest reaches of your store, thus encouraging customers to walk through the other departments of your store to get to these products (much like the grocery store described in the previous paragraph). You can also use strategically placed merchandise displays along your traffic flow route to encourage customer impulse buying. Make buying unplanned products the easiest possible thing to do for your customers and you will see an immediate increase in your sales (and your profits).

Conclusion. It is absolutely essential to the overall success of your store to develop an effective and efficient traffic flow pattern in your store. A properly designed traffic flow pattern will help ensure that customers are moved - in a comfortable, non-threatening manner - throughout all the departments of your store. Customers will then be exposed to all your product lines and they will be subtly encouraged to buy additional items that may not have been on their list of purchases. The result: increased sales, increased revenue, and increased profits.

E. THE STORE INTERIOR

This part of your store walk-through will demand objectivity and concentration. It is extremely important to continue your efforts to see things through a "fresh set of eyes." Before you actually start walking through the store pause and take a long look around the entire interior of your store.

Take some pictures that capture as much of the store's interior as possible. Then consider the following:

1. *Initial Impressions.* As you look around what are your initial, or first, impressions of the store? Do you see a store that is:

— Neat
— Clean
— Well organized
— Well stocked
— Well lighted
— Aisles free of obstacles
— Fixtures in good repair
— Interior adequately heated or air conditioned
— Any unpleasant odors or smells present in the store
— Interior adequately ventilated
— Walls, floors and carpeting in good repair
— Orderly and coordinated product displays
— Neutral color decor package
— Professionally prepared signage
— Customer-friendly feeling throughout the store
— Professional looking staff and sales associates
— Friendly and courteous staff and sales associates
— Knowledgeable staff and sales associates

   This initial look around the interior of your store is important because it should reinforce the importance of creating a positive first impression. After looking around are you left with a positive feeling?; a feeling that seems to "invite" you into the store to shop? Or, as you look around do you experience a feeling of confusion or disorganization? Review the list above and indicate which items create a positive or negative first impression. Then determine what can be done to correct any negative impressions. Remember, you should be striving to create a "Grand Opening" feeling in your store everyday.

2. *Store Fixtures.* Fixtures include all those units in the store that are used to hold or display your products. You should take some time to inventory the fixtures currently used in your store. This information will be useful if you decide at a later date to consider the purchase of new fixtures. We have provided a store fixture checklist for this purpose. The checklist will also let you know of the many different types of fixtures available to meet your retailing needs.

Store Fixture Inventory Checklist:
   1. Slatwall
   2. Pegboard
   3. Gondola

4. Wood fixtures

5. Brick 'N Board

6. Metal Wall Standards

7. Grid wire

8. Wire fixtures

9. Peg hooks (metal and plastic - what lengths and how many?)

10. Hangars
    a. "K-Mart" type specials
    b. Plastic hangars
    c. Wood hangars
    d. Metal hangars
    e. Other types

11. Glass showcases

12. Glass cubes

13. Wire cubes

14. Glass shelves

15. Wood shelves

16. Carpeted shelves

17. Pedestals

18. Acrylic fixtures

19. Metal garment fixtures:
    a. 2-way - 4-way - 6-way - box rack
    b. Rounders - Tri-rounders
    c. Hat racks
    d. Spiral racks
    e. Miscellaneous

20. Vendor provided fixtures:
    a. Wire
    b. Metal
    c. Wood
    d. Cardboard
    e. Plastic

FIXTURE EVALUATION:

As you walk-through your store and complete the inventory, you should also answer the following questions about your store's fixtures:

a. Are your store fixtures free of visible damage and in good repair?

b. Do you have an adequate number of fixtures available to hold and display your products?

c. Are you using the right fixture for the right job?
d. Do your fixtures create a feeling of organization and order?
e. Do any of your fixtures create obstacles to customer traffic flow?
f. Are you displaying the right product on the right fixture?
g. Are your fixtures too tightly grouped, discouraging or preventing easy customer browsing?
h. Do your fixtures seem to dominate the product displayed? (Are customers attracted to the product or to the fixture?)
i. Do your fixtures enhance the display of your products? Do they encourage customers to touch, feel, and BUY the products?
j. How many of your fixtures are new? Old? Used?
k. Are you aware of the wide variety of fixtures available to you for the display of your products?
l. Have you ever had a professional evaluation made of your fixtures by a store design specialist?

FIXTURE GUIDELINES:
1. Use the right fixture for the right job.
2. Keep all store fixtures in good repair.
3. Do not buy "cheap" fixtures - buy fixtures designed for your products in order to increase sales.
4. Fixtures should encourage customer contact with your products (see, touch, buy).
5. Arrange all fixtures in order to enhance traffic flow throughout your store.
6. Seek professional advice when in doubt about what fixtures to buy.
7. Invest in your store's success by purchasing the right fixtures at all times.
8. Inventory your fixtures at least once a year.
9. Fixtures should not dominate products - they should enhance product display.
10. Always have adequate fixtures to display your products.
11. Too many fixtures in one product area can create confusion and reduce "impulse" buying.
12. Learn to combine fixture systems that have compatible accessory hardware.
13. Consider the use of custom made fixtures if you have unique or non-traditional products for sale.
14. Choose a fixture company that has demonstrated experience in your field or product line.
15. Buy fixtures that are easily adaptable to multiple uses within your store.
16. Determine if your fixtures need updating or replacing - if in doubt, contact a design specialist.

The successful retail store of the 90's and beyond will be one that maximizes the use of quality product display fixtures. *(See Photos 1.6 and 1.7)* Properly selected and arranged fixtures are the tools that can dramatically improve the effectiveness of your product display - and increase sales, especially impulse sales. When considering the purchase of fixtures for your store do not make the often repeated mistake of buying "cheap." You will regret it. Spend time evaluating the type of product you sell and the type of customer you are trying to reach. Fixtures should be purchased for one primary reason: to successfully merchandise your products to your customers in the most effective and efficient way possible. If you have questions or are unsure of what to do, do not hesitate to contact a professional store design specialist to arrange for a comprehensive evaluation of your store's fixtures.

3. *Interior Cleanliness and Organization.* If you cannot spend another dollar to buy new fixtures or if you do not have any extra cash to paint or remodel your store interior, there is one thing you can still do - *right now* - to improve the overall image of your store (and it will cost you nothing): Clean and organize your store every day!!! Yes, it is absolutely true - "Cleanliness IS next to Godliness!" (at least in the retail industry . . .). Make sure your store is well-groomed and presentable prior to opening your doors for business every day. Complete all cleaning, vacuuming, dusting, polishing, product pick-up and stocking, sweeping, glass and window cleaning, trash pick-up, and maintenance BEFORE your store opens for business. Organize displays and merchandise not only prior to opening the store, but throughout the entire time the store is open. Always strive to create a positive, organized, and clean store interior. As you continue the store walk-through, evaluate the following items that may apply to your store:

— FLOORS/CARPETING. Are all your floors and carpeting cleaned, polished, or vacuumed? Are they free of debris and all trash?

— WALLS. Are the walls in good repair? Do any need painting or cleaning? Do they appear cluttered with disorganized or random product displays? Are the corners free of cobwebs?

— SIGNAGE. Are all the signs that appear in your store professionally prepared and visually attractive? Try not to use any hand-painted or hand-made signs in your store. Economical sign-making machines are available to accomplish this task. *(See Photo 1:37B)* Remember - you are trying to create a positive buying environment for your customers, one that reinforces the pride you have in your store and the products you sell.

— LIGHTING. Lighting for most retail stores has become both an art and a science. Proper lighting can create very strong (yet subtle) buying signals in the mind of a consumer. If you are not in a position to utilize the services of a professional store designer to provide a comprehensive package of recommendations for lighting your retail store, then consider the following suggestions:

... Make sure all existing lights are in good working order. Replace burned out bulbs or tubes immediately.

... Check the brightness of all lights in the store. Make sure your lighting does not cast shadows or create dark areas on or around your merchandise. On the other hand, ensure that your lighting is not too harsh or glaring making it difficult for your customers to see merchandise.

... Consider the use of subdued or indirect lighting techniques for appropriate products or merchandise displays.

... Make sure that all "special" product display areas are well lit, with sale prices or terms clearly marked.

... Make sure that all entrances and exits are properly and clearly lit.

... Parking lots and walkways to your store should be especially well lit to ensure the safety of your customers.

— BANNERS and STREAMERS. Banners and streamers, if used, should enhance the overall image of your store. Avoid using any banners or streamers that create a cluttered or disorganized appearance in your store. Banners or streamers advertising or promoting special sales should be professionally prepared and be removed immediately after the event.

— MANNEQUINS. Mannequins must always be in good repair and visually appealing. Remove or replace any mannequins that are worn, damaged, or obviously outdated (a mannequin designed for use in the 70's may look quite out of place in the 90's). Mannequins should be used to place a product in a real life buying context. Always exercise good judgment and good taste when using mannequins. When replacing old mannequins, consider purchasing new ones that are extremely versatile and flexible. The wise purchase and use of mannequins can greatly enhance your store's image and result in substantially increased sales.

— COUNTER/CASH WRAP AREAS. The counter and cashier areas should always be clearly visible and well marked. Nothing is more frustrating for a customer than to have items ready for purchase and not know where to go to pay for them. Make sure you have enough cashier areas (and staff) to handle the anticipated volume of customers - especially if you are having special sales or if it is a holiday season. Keep these areas clean and free of all merchandise except that which is being rung up for a customer. This will help avoid confusion and reduce the possibility for employee error.

— REST ROOMS. If you have rest rooms available for customer use, always make sure they are clean and well stocked - especially in peak or busy shopping times. Nothing will help create a more lasting, negative impression in the mind of a customer than to walk into a dirty, foul-smelling rest room. Do whatever is necessary to ensure your restrooms are cleaned on a regular basis throughout your store's hours of operation. Let your customers know you care about their well-being by practicing cleanliness in every part of your store's operation. A reminder - make sure your public restrooms comply with the requirements of the Americans With Disabilities Act.

— EMPLOYEE WORK AREAS/LUNCH ROOMS. Separate work and rest areas for your employees should always be clean and in good order, especially if any of these areas can be seen by the public. Train staff and employees to keep their areas well organized and free of clutter, especially those areas that may be located on the floor of the store (cash wrap or customer service areas, for example).

F. MERCHANDISE/PRODUCTS

INTRODUCTION

This phase of the walk-through will focus on your products and merchandise. You are in the retail business for one primary reason: to sell your products to the public in order to make a profit. Your store is the place where you can bring together your products (which you offer for sale), and the customers (those who will buy your products). A store without products is like a car without an engine - neither will get you where you want to go. Your evaluation will focus on the following:

1. *Merchandise available for sale.* Do you have adequate products on display and available to your customers? Do you have adequate product inventory available in the event of an unanticipated

increase in demand for your merchandise (sales, special seasonal offerings, etc.)? Do you have adequate and effective channels in place for reordering your products?

2. *Displaying Your Merchandise.* Are your product displays well organized? *(See Photo 1.27 & 1.28)* Are product displays strategically located throughout your store? Do all product displays have adequate merchandise available for customer purchase? Do your sales associates keep product displays replenished on a timely basis? Are your merchandise displays in good repair and visually appealing to the customer? Are price signs professionally prepared, accurate, and easily visible to the customer? Are the right products displayed on the right fixtures?

3. *Arranging and Ordering Merchandise.* Are your products arranged on the displays in an attractive, organized and customer-appealing manner? Do your sales clerks ensure that products removed from displays and not purchased are quickly returned to the display and properly arranged (this is especially important if your product line includes clothing)? Are empty product displays or shelves replenished on a timely basis? Are products moved to the front of the display ("front-facing") on a timely basis to ensure that products can be easily seen - and bought - by customers? Are your products arranged on displays, shelves, or racks by color, size or type?

4. *Paying For Merchandise.* After a customer has selected a product for purchase, can it be paid for easily and quickly? Are your cash registers and customer service areas clearly visible by the customers? Do you have an adequate number of register and wrap areas conveniently located throughout the store (especially during peak or busy times)? Do you have a sufficient number of sales associates available to handle customers who need assistance at the register areas? Do you offer customers convenient methods of paying for merchandise (cash, check, credit cards)?

Retailers concerned about quality customer service will offer shoppers a wide variety of payment options including check, credit cards, ATM cards, as well as cash.

5. *Stock Room Area.* Do you have an in-house stock room area? Is the stockroom area clean, neat and free of dangerous clutter and debris? Is the stockroom safe for employee use? Do your stockroom personnel come in contact with customers? If yes, are your stockroom personnel well groomed, properly dressed, and courteous to customers? Do you have an efficient system in place to get the merchandise from the stockroom to the customer in a timely manner (to avoid customer complaints and dissatisfaction)?

G. EMPLOYEES AND STAFF

INTRODUCTION

Your most important business asset is not product, it is human: your employees and staff. Nothing is more important to the long-term success of your store than the quality of your employees. This phase of the walk-through will focus on the human element of your store operation. Your evaluation should include the following:

1. *You, the Owner - Leading By Example.* You must be committed to the critically important principle of leading by example. Not only are you responsible for developing standards and guidelines for your employees to follow, you must be committed to practicing those standards and principles yourself.
2. *Establishing Goals and Objectives.* Your business success plan must include a clear and understandable presentation of the goals and objectives that you have developed for your store and employees. These goals must then be effectively communicated to your staff and employees (during the hiring process, during new employee orientation, during training sessions, during performance reviews).
3. *Employee Handbook.* Do you have an Employee Handbook of Policies and Procedures available? If not, see our chapter on developing and implementing an Employee Handbook for your store - Chapter 10.
4. *Employee Training and Development.* Do you have a formal training program in place for all employees? Is the training reviewed periodically and updated when necessary?
5. *Employee Communication.* Do you have effective methods in place to communicate information to all your employees? What methods do you use and how effective are those methods (memos, bulletin boards, regular staff and departmental meetings, company meetings, newsletters, etc.)?
6. *Employee Compensation and Benefits.* Do you have specific compensation and benefit programs in place? Have you prepared job or position descriptions for all employees? Have you established performance review standards and a schedule for conducting employee reviews? Is your compensation package reviewed periodically to ensure it remains fair and competitive?

H. CUSTOMERS

INTRODUCTION.
Let's face it, you won't be in business very long without customers. It is vitally important that you periodically attempt to measure the buying attitude of your customers. Are they satisfied with your products, your prices, your employees, your service? This can be accomplished in a number of ways: customer survey profile, unofficial conversations with those who shop at your store, customer questionnaires, follow-up surveys after a purchase has been made. You should also consider the following in completing this phase of your store walk-through:

1. Customer Profile - Who Buys Your Product?
2. Commitment to Customer Service and Satisfaction - Words or Deeds?
3. Customer Feedback - Am I doing my job?
4. Customer Communication - Keeping in touch with your customers after the purchase?
5. Value Added - Providing service your competitors do not - Your competitive edge!

CHAPTER 6

TRAFFIC FLOW—
THE SECRET TO SELLING
MORE PRODUCTS

"Getting customers into your store simply means you've won a battle.
To win the war, you must get them to see, touch, and buy your products."
—Jerry Rasmus

46

INTRODUCTION

Have you ever had occasion to take a trip to an unfamiliar place without the benefit of a road-map? You end up on strange roads with almost no idea where to go or how to get there. You come to intersections and are not quite sure which way to turn; you encounter towns and are not quite sure if this is the right way or not. The trip becomes a bewildering and often frustrating experience. Without a good map and a well planned itinerary your trip has probably ended up a disaster.

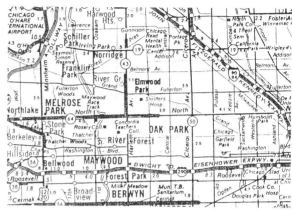

A good roadmap can help get you from point 'A' to point 'B' with ease and efficiency.

Many retail stores create the same kind of experience for shoppers every day. Consider the plight of the poor shopper who decides to visit a new store for the first time. The customer enters the store full of excitement and expectation looking forward to a positive shopping experience. The feelings of excitement and expectation are soon replaced with feelings of confusion and disappointment. Standing at the entrance the hapless shopper looks down and sees a six foot wide aisle leading from the front of the store directly to the rear of the store, feeling almost forced to follow the path of least resistance to a destination certainly not of their choosing. The poor shopper begins to feel just like the traveller without a roundmap - confused, frustrated, and probably a little angry. This is no doubt one store that will not rate a return visit.

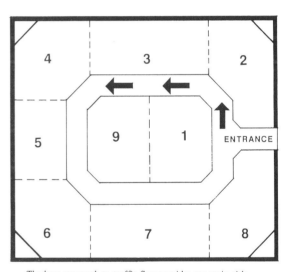

The loop approach to traffic flow provides one main aisle—designed by YOU—that will determine customer direction. You guide shoppers through all the departments of your store in a predetermined manner.

Winning retail stores win because they never forget why they are in business - to sell merchandise at a fair price, to make a profit, to make every shopper a repeat shopper, and to make every shopping experience a positive one. Winning retail stores understand the importance of traffic flow. This chapter will focus on defining and illustrating effective traffic flow concepts; describe how to create merchandise areas that sell product; and how to select and place the right fixtures for your products.

WHAT IS TRAFFIC FLOW?

Traffic flow is a retail concept that seeks to separate "customer space" from retail selling space. Customer space is that area a shopper uses to move from place to place in your store (often described as the customer's "walking space"). Retail selling space refers to those areas of your store reserved for the display and merchandising of your products. These are all the areas of your store you want to direct customers to. Effective traffic flow will provide opportunities for every shopper to be exposed to all the key merchandise areas of your store. Successful retail stores recognize the gold-mine of buying opportunities created through effective use of traffic flow patterns. Paying careful attention to your store's traffic flow pattern is one of the most important considerations you will make. Neglecting this critically important design element will result in dissatisfied customers, lost sales, and decreasing profits for you.

Traffic flow is the life blood of retail store health and success. It is like the blood that flows through your veins. The free and unobstructed flow of blood through your veins results in proper circulation and a feeling of health. If a blockage occurs, you begin to slow down and start to experience a deterioration of health. Failure to correct the problem could have disastrous results (heart attack, stroke, or even death).

The same is also true in retail store operations. Designing a traffic pattern that affords your shoppers a free and unobstructed path to all areas of your store will result in more sales, greater profits, and "good health." The opposite is also true. Time and time again I have visited stores where visual and physical blockages have impeded customers, preventing them (in some cases) from actually entering the store, or hindering them from seeing all the store's merchandise once they managed to enter the store. These obstructions to effective traffic flow will result in fewer sales, lower profits, and "poor health." If left uncorrected, you could end up facing disastrous results (loss of customers, declining profits, or even bankruptcy).

EFFECTIVE TRAFFIC FLOW: TWO OBJECTIVES

1. *Product Exposure.* Winning retail stores have designed effective traffic flow patterns for two primary reasons. The first is to provide every shopper with an opportunity to see between 80 - 100% of your merchandise areas every time they visit your store. *(See Photo 1.4)* Customers come into your store for a variety of reasons. Some may come in to shop for a specific item. They think they know exactly what they want and intend to go to that department or location, purchase the item, and leave. Others may come in your store not knowing for sure what they want. They may just be "looking around." In either case, effective traffic flow patterns will seek to direct all shoppers, in a predetermined manner, to every major merchandise or department of your store - *before they leave.* Your objective is to expose all your merchandise to every shopper on every visit. Consider this - IF THEY DON'T SEE IT, THEY CAN'T BUY IT!

Some of the most successful practitioners of this concept are today's modern department stores (Sears, K-Mart, Macy's, etc.) In most cases, the "basics" (linen, hosiery, undergarments, shoes) are located in the farthest reaches of the store. Why? The reason is obvious - to get every shopper, no matter what the reason may be they had for entering the store, to walk by as many of the other departments as possible before getting to the item they wanted. Retail department stores are masters at creating traffic flow patterns that move customers to as many different departments in the store as possible. The result: product, or merchandise, exposure (remember - if they don't see it, they can't buy it; or stated positively - if they do see it, they can buy it). This leads us to the second primary objective of effective traffic flow patterns - and it's the most important.

2. *Impulse Sales!* What is an "impulse sale"? Consider first the dictionary definition of *impulse*: a sudden inclination or tendency to act...a sudden driving force or influence. An impulse sale results when a shopper purchases an item as a result of a sudden force or influence upon the subconscious mind. The shopper, while walking through your store on the way to the parts or service department, *(See Photo 1.6)* passes through the t-shirt department, sees an attractive, eye-catching display of colorful t-shirts, and suddenly realizes how good that shirt would look on him (or her). If the traffic pattern in your store was simply a six foot aisle running from the store entrance directly to the parts or

service department, the shopper would not have been subconsciously motivated to consider making any other purchase. An effectively designed traffic flow pattern promotes impulse buying on the part of every shopper walking through your store.

If just 50% of all the shoppers that walk through your store end up purchasing one additional item at $5.00 with a 50% mark-up they did not intend to buy when they entered your store, what would that mean to your bottom line at the end of one year? Too good to be true? Absolutely not! The key is designing your store to take advantage of effective traffic flow patterns - patterns that comfortably move shoppers through all your merchandise areas and that promote shopper impulse buying.

Customers in the motorcycle and auto parts store industries are notorious for coming through the front

Effective traffic flow design will result in more impulse sales every day. More impulse sales will result in more cash and greater profits.

door and charging straight to the parts department. Why? Because they had no reason in the past to do otherwise. Over time, dealerships in this particular industry have encouraged customers to develop this habit simply because of the way the stores were designed. Dealers wanted the customers to go to the parts counter so the best way to accomplish this goal was to put in a wide aisle leading from the front of the store directly to the rear where, in most cases, the parts department was located. But this is no longer true. The new look in motorcycle and powersport stores for the 90's and beyond emphasizes effective traffic flow patterns designed to promote a wide variety of other merchandise while at the same time creating an "impulse buying" environment in the store. *(See Photo 1.4)*

If you are in the retail business it is absolutely imperative that you create a traffic flow pattern that gives customers a reason to walk through your store, to see, touch and feel all the products you have on display. Do you remember the popular movie *Field of Dreams?* Early in the film Kevin Costner heard a voice telling him, "Build the field and they will come." Well, he wasn't sure what was happening, but he built the baseball field, and guess what? The players came and they played. You may be very comfortable with the way things are in your store. But guess what? If you create the right traffic pattern, the shoppers will come - and they will BUY! They will buy their regular merchandise as they have always done; but now they will also start buying items they never considered before. Why? Because you gave them an opportunity to see and touch items they may have never known were even in your store. The result: more impulse sales and greater profits.

CONDITIONED RESPONSE

Fortunately, many shoppers are conditioned to respond to certain basic store design elements. One such response is to stay within visible lines or boundaries. Beginning in grade school we were constantly told to "stay in line." As adults this is still true. Whether you visit your bank, a movie theatre, or an airport, you are either told or directed to "stay in line." Effective traffic flow takes advantage of this conditioned response. Today, stores are designed with "built-in" or predetermined paths that customers will follow almost without thinking. This technique is accomplished by providing customers with their own designated "walking space" or aisles, specifically designed to direct them through every major merchandise area of the store. Most shoppers are not even conscious this is happening. They simply respond to their environment.

There are some other conditioned responses most shoppers exhibit which may also be used to your advantage in designing an effective traffic flow pattern for your store. One of them is the tendency to move to the right. If confronted with an intersection and a choice to go either right or left, most people will move to the right (we read from left to right and the majority of people are right handed). Being aware of this tendency will help you to more effectively present your merchandise, thus increasing your potential for more impulse sales. Most people are also conditioned to obey signs or signals and to respond to them in a positive way when part of an overall traffic flow pattern. As a retailer you have the ability to capitalize on these types of conditioned responses through effective and creative traffic flow planning. The result will be increased sales and increased profits.

TEST YOUR REGULAR SHOPPERS

Take a moment and watch your regular customers as they enter the store. Where is the first place they generally go? In most cases, they will proceed to their favorite department, and take the path of least resistance to get there. (When I enter a department store, for example, the first place I go to is the sporting goods section...and I will try to avoid all the other departments, if possible, to get there.) Shoppers are creatures of habit. Effective traffic flow design seeks to break old shopping habits in a non-threatening way, and replace them with new shopping habits that will result in more opportunities for impulse buying decisions to be made. As a retailer, you have the ability to direct customers to any part of your store, and to expose them to whatever merchandise you desire, as they walk through your store. This is the essence of effective traffic flow design. If you are not taking advantage of these techniques you are losing sales every day your store is open for business. Determining the right traffic flow pattern is critically important. We'll examine two approaches used by retailers today and consider their advantages and disadvantages.

TYPES OF TRAFFIC FLOW PATTERNS

Most specialty retail stores today - from the single unit to small chains of ten or more stores - will utilize one of two basic traffic flow patterns. The grid (or perpendicular) and the loop. The grid method of traffic flow design is a common traffic pattern in most single unit stores, whether large or small. Typically, stores using this approach to traffic flow will arrange merchandise in a perpendicular, or grid, manner beginning at the front entrance to the store. This creates the effect of having multiple avenues or grids through which the customer may walk while shopping. When standing at the entrance to a store using this approach, most shoppers must choose one path from among many to do their shopping.

Since most shoppers are already "conditioned" to make choices that offer the least resistance to existing habits, they will normally pick an aisle or path that contains their favorite merchandise or products. They will walk down that aisle and if they don't find what they are looking for, they will turn around and leave the store. The result - lost opportunities for impulse sales. In this situation, the customer is in control.

This approach to traffic flow and merchandise design may also impede sales by creating subliminal walls (or barriers). Since fixtures and merchandise are usually displayed in long rows, shoppers in one row may never see the products in adjacent rows because they don't like the idea of pushing through racks of merchandise to get from one aisle to another - it's much easier to just walk back out the aisle and leave the store, or go directly to nearest register and pay for an item and leave. These long runs of merchandise and fixtures create what is called the *railroad effect*. If the fixtures and merchandise run parallel for any distance, the items tend to "disappear" as the customer walks that particular aisle.

The grid approach to traffic flow design can be seen in hundreds of stores today. Stores designed for the 90's and beyond, however, are

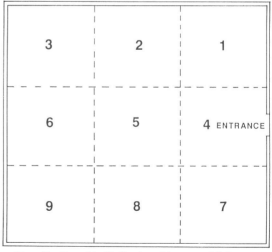

The grid pattern of traffic flow is used by many retail stores. Note the numerous "main aisles" available to your customers. Which one will they choose?

beginning to use an approach that offers the retailer much more flexibility, creativity, and potential for greatly increasing sales and profits. This approach is called *the loop*.

THE LOOP APPROACH

Effective traffic flow design seeks to accomplish a number of important goals for the retailer. They include:

1. To create a "loop", or race track style of traffic flow.
2. To delineate customer walk space from retail merchandise space.
3. To create merchandise focal points.
4. To move customers through all the major merchandise areas of your store.
5. To expose 80 - 100% of your merchandise to every customer walking through your store.
6. To provide the correct fixtures for displaying your products and merchandise.
7. To utilize correct merchandising techniques for all your products.
8. To enhance your opportunities for increased impulse sales.
9. To provide for more rapid merchandise turn-over.
10. To achieve increased sales, increased profits, and improved customer service.

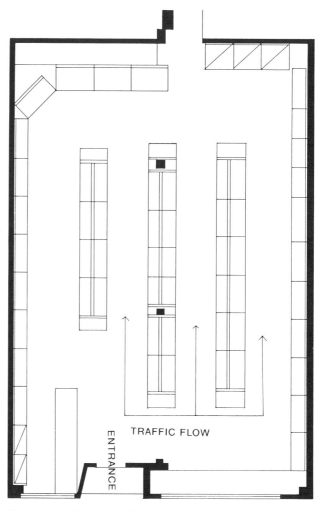

Note the many aisle choices available to customers in the grid pattern design as they enter the store. In this situation, the customer controls his path and direction.

Effective traffic flow design begins with the *loop* approach. The concept of the loop approach is a simple, but effective one. It combines a knowledge of the conditioned responses of most shoppers with creative design techniques and the result is a pattern of traffic flow that accomplishes the two most important goals discussed so far: (1) To expose 80 - 100% of your merchandise to every shopper walking through your store; and (2) To create impulse buying opportunities throughout every department of your store.

Most retailers will be able to consider implementing the loop traffic pattern utilizing existing retail space. I have visited few retail store operations where this technique could not be readily adapted. The loop, or race track, design starts at the front door and gently guides the customer to move to the right. The goal is to lead each customer through every major merchandise area of your store. How is this accomplished? By providing a clearly defined "customer walk space" throughout your store. You will create four to six foot wide aisles that will guide customers as they walk through your store. These aisles will serve as your own "yellow brick road," effectively guiding shoppers to each department of your store while at the same time providing opportunities to showcase new or seasonal merchandise at predetermined areas throughout the

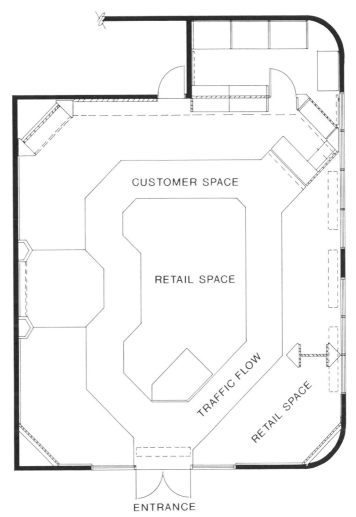

The loop approach to traffic flow creates a customer walking space and directs (or guides) the shopper throughout the store exposing them to new departments and new merchandise. Your goal: more impulse sales!

store. By utilizing proper fixtures and creative merchandising techniques, you will be able to create many additional customer buying opportunities throughout your store. When customers can see more products, they will buy more products.

BREAKING OLD SHOPPING HABITS

The loop pattern seeks to break old shopping habits. By opening up your retail space to the shopper, you have effectively exposed more of your products, thus increasing your opportunities for additional sales. The loop approach is designed to break shoppers of the old habit of walking into your store, going down their favorite aisle, and then leaving. The loop nudges them along a predetermined path, while at the same time creatively displaying new and different merchandise for purchase. The customer may have entered your store with the intent of going directly to a particular department, but in order to get there, the shopper must now walk through several other departments, each of which is displaying new products for that customer to purchase.

I'm a runner. Every time I need a new pair of running shoes I go to my favorite sporting goods store. It used to be very easy to buy a pair of running shoes in that store. The shoes used to be on display just as you entered the store so I would walk in, try on a few pairs, make my selection, pay for them, and leave. Well, a few years ago this store changed a few things. They instituted the loop approach to traffic flow. Now when I enter the store (and I still do all my shopping there), a wide, spacious aisle guides me through the store to the shoe department (which is now located in the rear of the store). To get to the running shoes I must now pass through the t-shirt department, the running shorts and accessories department, the watch department, the pro-sports hat department, and the fitness and exercise department. Guess what happens every time I visit this store? You're right - by the time I get to the running shoes, I have seen at least six other items I didn't think about but suddenly realized I needed, or I have seen three or four "specials" on display in various aisles on my way to the running shoes. The result - I walk up to the register with my running shoes and at least two or three other items I had not originally intended to purchase. These other items are my "impulse buys." Think about how these types of sales will add up over the course of a week, or a month, or a year. This is exactly how the loop approach to traffic flow design was intended to work - and it does!

CONSIDER ALL THE ANGLES!

When designing the loop pattern for your store several factors should be considered. First, remember that the aisles must be considered "customer space." *(See Photo 1.7)* Do not put merchandise, boxes, or fixtures in this space. If you do, you'll create obstacles and distractions, causing your customers to watch every step they take rather than looking at your merchandise displays or "special offers."

Second, you should try to use 45-degree angles when turning corners in the loop pattern. It's a smoother transition than using a 90-degree turn and it enables you to to create focal points in corners where two walls meet. This technique creates what is called a "sight line" - a customer's line of vision as they walk the aisle in search of their desired item. This "sight line" will draw the customer's attention away from the main aisle toward the wall which contains merchandise on display. Using the more gentle 45-degree angles will also cause customers to continue on the loop even after they have made their primary purchase. This will enable you to expose the shopper to more merchandise which, in turn, will create more impulse buying opportunities before they leave the store. *(See Photos 1.4 and 1.9)*

Third, the loop concept will create equal value among all your departments, offering the shopper shallower but longer display areas without "railroading" the customer past displays. Each department now becomes another opportunity you have to sell additional merchandise to the customer. The loop guides the customer to each department or merchandise area; your fixtures are used to attractively display your products; and creative merchandising techniques will promote impulse buying. The loop concept opens the door for more sales and greater profits.

CAPPING THINGS OFF

Utilizing the loop concept may also make it possible for you to double the end cap capacity on your gondolas. Replacing long, boring runs with smaller aisles and more end caps is a great way to stimulate impulse buying because most of the end caps are accessible from the main aisle. *(See Photo 1.10)* A shopper walking to a particular department will probably pass by several end cap displays, thus creating additional opportunities for impulse purchases. Professional retail journals estimate that up to 65 - 75% of all sales made in today's retail market are impulse buys. Men in particular are notorious impulse buyers. Most men can be easily "coaxed" into bringing home just one more item if you design your store properly. I speak from experience. When my wife calls the office and asks me to pick up a gallon of milk on my way home, I immediately check to see if I have an extra ten or fifteen dollars with me - because I know when I walk into the grocery store that's what I'll end up spending. Why? Impulse buying! Women shoppers, on the other hand, will take time to "shop" their way around the loop to make sure they don't miss any bargains or unadvertised sales. Women are great impulse buyers too, they just take a little more time than men. If you are not taking advantage of these opportunities in your store you are losing sales every day. Maybe now is the time to reconsider your approach to traffic flow - it may be time to take your store from the 60's and 70's look into the 90's and beyond.

THE LOOP: HOW TO IMPLEMENT

The loop concept can be achieved in most stores with a minimum of expense and disruption to your retail sales efforts. On the other hand, if you are considering building a new store or remodeling an existing store, you may want to budget enough money to make sure you can create an effective, attractive, and sales-generating loop concept. Your choices will be limited only by your imagination, existing store limitations, and your budget.

The easiest and least expensive way to create a loop effect - if you have vinyl or concrete floors - is to use 3M tape (product #471-2″) and apply it directly to your floor. *(See Photo 1.11)* Sit down and figure out where you want your customer "paths" to be. Then determine how you want to rearrange your merchandise or products around the loop aisle. Depending on the size of your store and the type of products you sell, you may be able to accomplish the project in one day, or it may take several. The important thing to remember is that the loop concept works - it will be worth the time and effort it takes to make the necessary changes to your store.

If your store is fully carpeted, you may be able to lay out on the carpet the loop you feel is best for your store. The next step would be to cut through the carpet following the outline of your traffic loop and install vinyl tiles. This approach has often been called the "yellow brick road" technique. It is important to choose a tile color that is complementary with your carpet and the store's decor. I would strongly recommend that you hire a professional installer to apply the tiles. You want to make sure that your store's interior is as attractive as possible to your customers. The loop effect is too important to your store to be content with anything less than a professional job.

Another option to consider is installing new tiles (ceramic or commercial grade vinyl) if you were already planning to put down a new floor. Be sure to choose two contrasting colors, one for the main customer aisle and the other for the perimeter and islands that will be created as you design the traffic flow pattern. Clothing and accessory areas should be carpeted if possible in order to create a customer-friendly shopping environment. Tiles make an effective choice for the customer loop section. Remember to place all fixtures at a 45-degree angles to the main customer aisle no matter what approach you may end up taking in creating the actual loop in your store. This technique will ensure that all your merchandise receives maximum exposure as customers follow the traffic loop. Be sure to replace any fixtures that look out of place or are not presentable. This is especially important for those fixtures most visible on the main aisle.

IT'S A WRAP

Take a good look at your store. What approach to customer traffic flow are you using? If you have completed your store walk-through discussed in Chapter 5, you should have noted the shopping habits of your regular customers. Are you utilizing every opportunity in your store to expose 80 - 100% of your merchandise to your customers every time they shop in your store? If not, then you should give very serious consideration to implementing the loop concept in your store. Decide what approach is best for you given your budget, your products, and any physical limitations your store may have. Then - JUST DO IT! The loop concept can help you accomplish two critically important goals:

1. Make more products available to your customers.
2. Create more impulse buying opportunities for every customer.

The bottom-line result will be more sales, greater profits, and more satisfied customers. The loop traffic flow concept works. Put it to work for you today.

1.1–Store exteriors can help create a positive first impression as well as enhance your store's image.
A powerful, professional exterior is your personal invitation to "Come on in and shop!"

1.2–Choosing the right exterior materials can set your store apart from the competition. Note the strong, positive first impression made by this exterior store sign.

1.3–Exterior awnings not only add a touch of class to your store, they can also serve to protect your products—and your customers—from adverse weather conditions.

1.4–Effective traffic flow design should result in more product on display for your customers. Remember— "the more they see, the more they can buy."

1.5–Combining effective traffic flow techniques with the right fixture for the right product will result in a store that appears to have ample merchandise to meet customer needs. Note the positive shopping image created by placing the fixtures at a 45-degree angle.

1.6–"Billboard" your fixtures and products to achieve maximum effectiveness (low at the aisle, higher in the middle, and highest at the wall). Focal points at the back wall will serve as magnets that "pull" your customers from the main aisles to other shopping areas of the store.

1.7–This photo illustrates effective lighting techniques, creative use of merchandise fixtures, and a strong traffic flow pattern—all keys to the successful merchandising of your products. The result: increased sales and increased profits.

1.8–Fixtures placed at a 45-degree angle will help create sight lines to the merchandise on the wall.

1.9–The traffic loop and placing fixtures at 45-degree angles will help expose more of your merchandise to the shopper. Note the effective use of garment fixtures to showcase this retailer's clothing merchandise.

1.10–This retailer combined an effective use of the loop design of traffic flow with end cap product displays to expose the shopper to more product.

1.11–Establishing an effective traffic flow pattern can be as easy as a roll of 3-M tape — specifically, #471-2″. Note the use in this photograph to mark off the customer walk area.

1.12–Quality store fixtures are the props that support your merchandise. We'll say it again — use the right fixture for your products. The wrong fixture will cost you valuable sales. Effective merchandising begins with the right fixture.

1.13–Going back in time? Get out of the 60's and 70's and into the 90's and beyond! Brick and board fixtures are still used by many retailers today and the result is usually lost sales. Why? Because they lack the flexibility and adaptability of more contemporary store fixtures available today.

1.14–Have you responded to the call for change? This *Store of the Year* did and sales skyrocketed! Your customers ask for a clean, well-stocked, and well lit store-it's up to you to give it to them.

1.15A & 1.15B–These two photos illustrate an effective use of glass cubes to display merchandise. Note how these highly popular fixtures won't hide your products. In addition, they make more retail space available because they are vertical in design instead of horizontal.

1.16–This photo illustrates an effective use of both glass showcases and glass towers to display merchandise.

1.17–Mannequins - your "silent salesmen." When used, mannequins should always be fully dressed to achieve maximum effect.

1.18–Is it real or is it...? Soft, flexible mannequins can make your customers stop and take a second look.

1.19–This photo illustrates how soft mannequins can create a sense of action and excitement when used to display certain types of products. They are available in a variety of sizes from child to adult, male or female, and you can choose from grey, black, or creme colors.

1.20–Note how pedestal risers can help create a buying "mood" when used effectively. They are available in a wide range of sizes to meet most merchandising needs. Don't forget to combine with decorative lighting and you'll create a dynamic merchandise display that will attract customer attention.

1.21–This powersports retailer demonstrates how a triple-tiered display can add visual excitement to your merchandising efforts. Adding a soft mannequin to the display (when appropriate) can increase overall effectiveness. Be sure to change the display frequently to keep it fresh and exciting.

1.22–To be a successful retailer in today's consumer-conscious buying environment you need to adopt the attitude that every day is "Grand Opening" day. Notice how this powersports retailer invites customers to "Come on in and shop!" by creating a visually exciting and dynamic merchandise display at the entrance to the store.

BEFORE

1.24A–
When your merchandise is low, front-face and spread-to-fill all gaps on the shelves. Notice the difference in appearance between the "before" and "after" photographs.

AFTER
1.24B–

1.23–Successful merchandising can be learned! Notice how this retailer *front-faces* his merchandise in order to create a "full-look" on the shelves.

1.25–This photo illustrates the effective use of color-blocking merchandise vertically. Also, learn to take advantage of manufacturer packaging for your shelving displays. Put as much product on your shelves and fixtures as possible— don't keep merchandise in your stockroom unless you have to.

1.27–This photo illustrates a definite merchandising negative—never mix products (in this case, tires and apparel). Learning some basic merchandising techniques can dramatically increase your sales and profits. It's worth your time and effort!

1.26–This display emphasizes the benefits of color blocking apparel merchandise. Customers are affected by color, style, and price (in that order).

1.28–Notice the powerful visual effect created by this retailer's skillful merchandising efforts. Learning to create that "Grand Opening" look every day in your store will keep your customers excited—and more importantly, keep them buying more of your products.

1.29–Focal points that utilize slatwall can break up a rather boring looking long wall and make it exciting. Lighted duratrans boxes on the face can tell your product story.

1.30–Seasonal merchandising using focal points can be very successful. Focal points are especially effective for special sales, introducing new products, and holiday sales.

1.31–Focal points should be visible from a distance. Note in this photo how visually strong the focal point is and how it serves as a magnet to attract the customer's attention and bring them to that part of the store.

1.32–Using glass showcases as a cash wrap counter is common practice with many retailers. You should be aware that merchandise contained in these glass showcases typically "dies" because sales clerks are reluctant to hold up others that may be in line to pay for merchandise.

1.33–Cash wrap and parts counters should be clean, free of vendor fixtures, and ready to serve your customers.

1.34–Cash wraps counters provide you with an excellent opportunity to make a final "positive impression" with your customers. Make the most of these opportunities.

1.35–A lighted valance is a must for your wall gondolas. Don't rely on your ceiling light fixtures to adequately illuminate this type of fixture. Effective lighting techniques will help draw customers to all merchandise areas of the store. Creative end cap and signage merchandising techniques will prove very effective in telling your product story.

1.36–Products should be raised off the floor when possible. This communicates to your customers a respect for your products and will also reduce the possiblity of product damage.

1.37A–Sign holders are also a must for displaying prices and other shopper information— throw away your tape dispenser and thumb tacks.

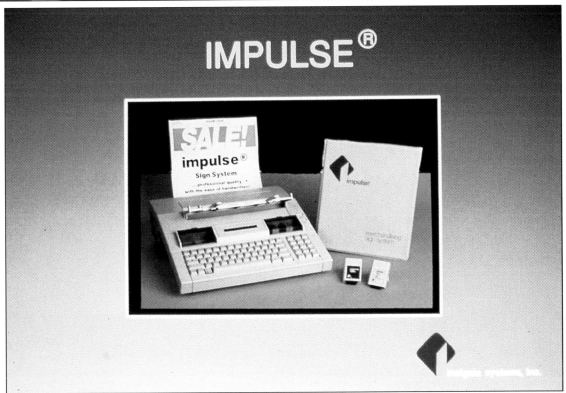

1.37B–The Insignia Sign Machine can help you create professional looking signs throughout your store.

1.38–Enhance your store's image by using neutral colors for your fixture backdrops. Fixtures should not dominate your product—they should enhance the product. Customers are interested in your products, not your fixtures.

1.39–The service counter area provides you with an excellent opportunity to show your customers additional products, thus creating the possibility for more impulse sales. Studies have shown that impulse sales can add up to 65 to 70% of your total sales—
if you practice effective merchandising and display techniques throughout your store.

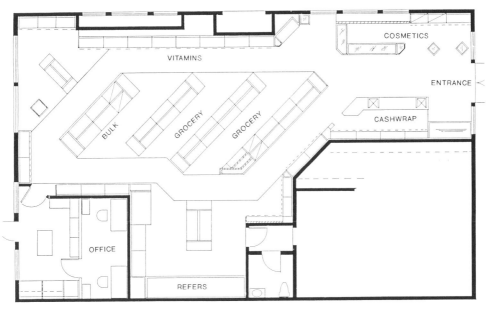

Illustration 6.1—Health food store space plan highlighting the use of 45-degree angles for product fixtures. Note the smooth transition for turning corners created by placing the fixtures at 45-degree angles.

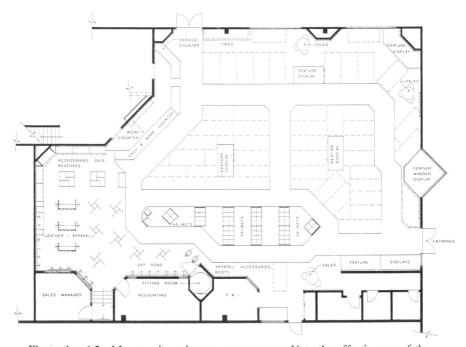

Illustration 6.2—Motorcycle and power sports store. Note the effective use of the loop traffic flow design. Customers are guided to all areas of the store, thus increasing the opportunity for additional impulse sales.

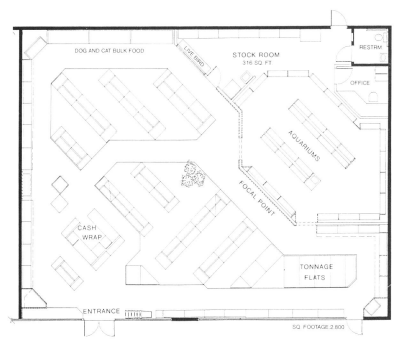

Illustration 6.3—Pet store space plan illustrating loop traffic design, 45-degree angle for fixtures, and placement of merchandise departments in the store.

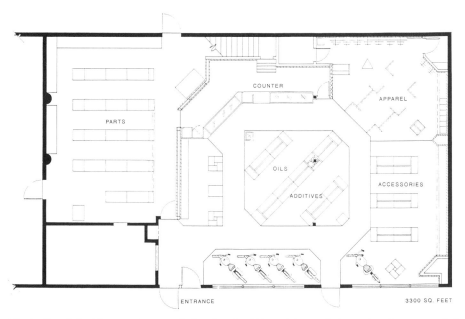

Illustration 6.4—Motorcycle store design for the 90's and beyond. Note the placement of the parts department and the cash & customer area. This store design emphasizes the loop traffic flow pattern and a strong display area at the entrance to the store.

CHAPTER 7

FIXTURES: HOW TO SHOWCASE YOUR PRODUCTS AND INCREASE YOUR SALES

"The most effective fixture I know of is the one that causes a customer to buy a product."
—Jim Rasmus

INTRODUCTION

Imagine what your home would be like without any furniture. You come home after a hard day at work, open the front door, and walk into an empty living room. No sofa, no chairs, no coffee table, no bookcases, no carpet, no curtains - nothing. The same is true for your kitchen, your bedroom, your den, your bathroom, every room is without furniture. Now imagine all your possessions—books, lamps, dishes, pictures, pots & pans—sitting on the floor. Not much of a home is it? Now imagine what your store would look like without any fixtures. Fixtures are to a store what furniture and accessories are to a house. A store without fixtures is an unfinished store.

Fixtures are all those items that are used in a store to accept, hold, arrange, and display your merchandise and products. Fixtures are the resources that help you showcase all that you have for sale in your store. Remove the fixtures from your store and your store ceases to function. All store fixtures have one basic purpose - to help you sell merchandise more effectively and efficiently. It is important, therefore, to give careful attention to your store's fixtures. This chapter will focus on the qualities to look for in selecting store fixtures and describe the types and uses of store fixture systems available today.

FIXTURES: PLANNING AND BUDGETING

The ideal time to consider your fixture needs is when your store is being planned. Selecting the right fixture should be coordinated with your traffic flow design. You will need to determine which fixture system is most effective for the type of merchandise and products you sell. Fixtures should also be evaluated on other qualities such as flexibility, function, adjustability, size, style, quantity, finish and, of course, price. If you are in the initial planning stages for your store then now is time to give serious consideration to these factors. If your store is already up and running then you may need to give consideration to a store redesign or remodel. Selecting the right fixtures for your store must be part of an overall store design plan. If it is not, you may end up with fixtures not suitable for your store's merchandise and products, resulting in lost sales and lower profits. *(See Photo 1.12)* Careful planning of your fixture needs and matching those needs with the right fixture will prove to be time well invested. Once you have developed your store traffic flow pattern the next step is to determine the right fixture to meet your needs.

Planning & budgeting in advance can ensure that you'll have the necessary funds available for replacing old and outdated fixtures. Plan to set aside 1 to 3% of gross revenues for this purpose.

An important element in the selection of the right fixture for your store is price. In fact, when I talk with store owners or managers, the number one consideration they mention when discussing the purchase of fixtures is price. Although this is understandable, I believe function and purpose are, in the long run, far more important considerations than price when considering fixture needs. Because of this, we strongly recommend that store owners plan in advance for replacing old and outdated fixtures.

How? By setting aside on a systematic basis one to three percent of gross revenues for the specific purpose of updating fixtures, repairs and employee training. Again, planning and budgeting must be part of the store owner's long-range goals.

THE RIGHT FIXTURES MEAN INCREASED SALES

The effective merchandising of your products requires that you use the right fixtures. Fixtures are the "props" that help set the stage for effective product merchandising. *(See Photo 1.12)* The days of the old "brick and board" stores are over. You remember those stores - they opened with nothing more than wood shelves resting on cinder block supports for the display of merchandise and products. These "fixtures" have remained in place in certain stores since opening day and are still used by some retailers today. I recently completed a store design in which the owner told me he inherited "brick and board" fixtures from the previous owner who had them installed when the store opened fifteen years ago. Some things are still slow to change.

How long has it been since you took a careful look at the fixtures in your store? *(See Photos 1.12 & 1.13)* How long has it been since you evaluated the effectiveness of the fixtures in your store? If it's been two or more years, then you are probably loosing sales on a daily basis. Using outdated or improper fixtures will prevent you from presenting your products to customers in the most effective manner possible. The result: fewer impulse sales in particular, and fewer sales in general. Using improper or outdated fixtures hinders your ability to adjust to product changes or to respond to seasonal and promotional display opportunities.

One of the most difficult problems I encounter when discussing fixture needs with store owners or managers is the resistance to change. All too frequently I hear the following: "I've had these fixtures for ten years and I don't see why I need to change them now." Really? Truly successful stores in the retail industry have always been marked by an ability to be on the cutting edge of change. Those that are not fail. Take Sears for example. For decades Sears was the leader in the retail store industry. Then an interesting thing began to happen about 15 years ago. New stores started to emerge in the marketplace. Stores characterized by innovation, new products, customer service, and competitive pricing. Speciality stores catering to specific customer needs and wants began to dominate the market. Sears failed to respond to the changing face of retailing in the 80's. They were soon replaced as the nation's leading retailer by upstarts like K-Mart and Wal-Mart. My point is simple: Successful retailers respond to change or they will fail. You may have been doing things the same for the past ten years and survived, but the important question is this: How successful could you have become if you had responded to changing customer needs by creating a store environment that excites, motivates, and produces more sales?

That's the goal of fixturing. To help you display and sell more merchandise. If you're content with your ten year old fixtures then I encourage you to take off your rose colored glasses and visit some of your competitors. Especially those that are growing and taking more and more of your customers. Why are they growing and you are not? In most cases the answer is because they are on the cutting edge of change and are willing to invest in making their store more responsive to the customer demands and needs of the 90's and beyond. Instead of buying another new car, or taking a third vacation to the Bahamas, or buying another high-tech electronic device, the cutting-edge retailers of the 90's are investing in their store's success. This means they are planning and budgeting for the continuous replacement of old and outdated fixtures. The retailer concerned with long-term success and growth does not view this as simply another "expense." The cutting-edge retailer of the 90's views this as an investment in the future success of his store. Is this your attitude? If not, it should be. When considering store fixtures, several factors are important. They are summarized below.

FIXTURES: BASIC CONSIDERATIONS

1. *Function*. Careful consideration must be given to what a specific fixture will do for you in your store in order to effectively display your products. Will this particular fixture help create more buying opportunities? Will it promote greater impulse buying by customers? (Example: You would probably not use glass cubes to display hammers. You would use peg board with peg hooks or a gondola with metal shelving.)

2. *Flexibility*. When considering a fixture, ask yourself if it has more than one possible use in your store. Try to invest in fixtures that will give you the opportunity for multiple uses.

3. *Adjustability*. Effective fixtures should have the ability to adjust in height, width, and sometimes depth. When evaluating clothing racks, for example, be sure that the merchandising arms are adjustable up and down and that you have other snap-on attachments to adapt to smaller size items. Metal, wire, or wood gondolas should have the ability to adjust shelves in small increments.

4. *Size*. Size is important since you won't want to choose a fixture that overpowers your products or your store motif. Customers eyes should be attracted to your products, not your fixtures.

5. *Style*. It is very important to consider the look, or style, of the fixture in order to conform to the type of business you have as well as the type of products you offer for sale. Style of fixture helps set the tone and "feel" of your store for your customers. The style of the fixtures you select should serve to enhance the overall image of your store rather than detract from it.

6. *Style Color and Finish*. The color or finish of your fixtures should serve to draw attention to your products and merchandise. The best finish is often one that is neutral. Neutral colors or finishes are best suited to serve as the backdrop for the products you place on them. Neutral colors also provide the greatest flexibility when your products change. It becomes very costly and time consuming if you have to repaint your fixtures.

7. *Quantity*. The number of fixtures you need will be determined by the volume of products you plan to display, the design of your store, your traffic flow pattern, and the inventory you plan to carry. If you are new to retailing I would recommend that you consider securing the services of a professional store designer to assist you in making these determinations. In addition, you may want to discuss your needs with your product suppliers and vendors. Another good source of information might also be your fixture vendor. However, you should be aware that most fixture vendors will try to sell you as many fixtures as possible - after all that's how they make their money. A professional store designer

tends to be much more objective in determining your needs. Other factors to keep in mind when considering how many fixtures you may need are: (1) seasonality of the products sold; (2) product turnover; (3) special promotions or sales planned throughout the year; (4) anticipated holiday sales; (5) inventory on hand; (6) type and size of merchandise sold; and (7) your budget.

8. *Price*. Although we realize that most store owners/managers will tend to put price first on the list of importance when considering fixture purchases, experience has taught me that price should never be the deciding factor. The most important factor is making sure the fixture is the right one for your store, your products, and your customers. Purchasing the wrong fixture simply because it is cheaper is a decision that will always come back to haunt you. Invest in the right fixture and you will realize both short and long-term benefits (more impulse sales, growing profits, and more new customers). I understand that cash flow may be a critical factor at times and will be the determining factor in your fixture purchase decisions. In those situations, it may be best to consider buying the right fixtures, but fewer of them. Proper budgeting and setting aside one to three percent of your gross sales revenue on a consistent basis is the best approach to solving this dilemma.

FIXTURE SELECTION

Before I describe and illustrate some of the most common types of fixturing systems available, let me take a moment to discuss some of the options available to you when it comes time to shop for your fixtures.

1. *Using a professional store designer/planner*. The best approach to fixture selection is to work with a professional store designer/planner. Not only can this individual help you with the overall design of your store and its interior, the store designer can integrate your fixture needs with the other design factors unique to your store. The professional store designer can make sure that the fixtures selected will fit in with your traffic flow pattern, your flooring, your decor package, and your store's image or theme. In addition, the store designer can generally shop your fixture needs around in order to secure the best selection and price for you. The services provided by the professional store designer will save you a lot of valuable time and effort and will enable you to focus on those tasks most important to you - operating and managing your store.

2. *Using vendor supplied fixtures*. If you are not in a position to use the services of a professional store designer, you might consider using fixtures provided by your product vendors. In most instances, these fixtures are "free" and are designed to display the specific products of that vendor. You might be thinking "If I can get free fixtures, why not take them?" Let me tell you why. First, the vendor supplied fixtures generally have a limited product use. They are not easily adaptable for other products or merchandise not provided by that vendor. Second, these types of fixtures usually stick out like a sore thumb - they are not coordinated with any other fixtures in your store and they are not coordinated with your store's interior decor. In some stores this may not be a problem. In most stores, it is a serious problem. Third, if you take every free fixture available you'll end up with a store full of fixtures that are not compatible, look totally out of place, and create a sense of disorganization.

I recently completed a store walk-through for a small vacuum and sewing store. The store was divided in half with vacuums and supplies occupying the left side of the store and sewing machines and supplies on the right. At the end of the vacuum cleaner side was a large promotional display fixture featuring a particular name brand of vacuum cleaner. The display featured a life-size picture of what looked like a race car driver that completely dominated the fixture. It looked completely out of place in the store and detracted from the overall appearance created by the other product displays and fixtures. This is a common occurrence in many retail stores. Keep in mind that "free" is not always best for you or your store. If you must use vendor supplied fixtures, make sure they fit into your store's image and decor. Don't use them if they will detract from your image or appearance.

3. *Doing it yourself.* If your budget is too tight to consider any other alternatives, you can take time away from your other duties and contact fixture vendors yourself. You can request catalogs and price lists and do the shopping and selection yourself. Unless you are a fixture "expert" you run the risk of making your fixture selections based most often on price only. You may not have the expertise to know the differences between types and styles of fixtures. The result may be the purchase of a fixture that is not right for your store or your merchandise. This option will also require a considerable amount of your time and effort. Locating fixture vendors, calling them, ordering catalogs, reading through the catalogs, trying to select the right fixtures, ordering the fixtures, waiting for the fixtures, worrying about shipping problems, receiving wrong or damaged fixtures, establishing credit or payment terms, resolving conflicts...all of these items can take enormous amounts of your time. This means that you cannot do what you do best - operate and manage your store. If this is the only option available to you, however, I recommend you plan well in advance of your actual fixture needs.

4. *Working with local fixture vendors.* You may be fortunate enough to be located in an area that has fixture vendors or suppliers. If so, you may be able to call them and ask to have an account representative come to your store to discuss your needs. Again, this option will require a great deal of your personal time and effort. You will, however, be working with a live human being rather than a catalog or a telephone order clerk. If you are unable to work with a professional store designer in assessing your fixture needs and options, this may be your next best alternative.

The remainder of this chapter will illustrate and describe some of the basic types of fixtures and fixture systems available to meet the needs of most small to medium-sized retailers.

BASIC TYPES OF RETAIL FIXTURES

1. *Slatwall.* Slatwall is one of the most versatile fixture systems available to the retailer. *(See Photos 1.8, 1.6, 1.18)* Slatwall is generally available in large 4' by 8' sections and is placed on your walls much like a sheet of plywood paneling. Slatwall contains grooves into which you can place metal arms that are used to display your products. Slatwall material is usually made from medium density fibre board and is available in plywood, metal, and high density foam or plastic. Prices vary widely according to quantity purchased and quality. For most retail stores, 3" or 4" on center grooves will accommodate a wide variety of products. Slatwall is available in many types of finishes including unfinished (you must

paint), mealtime (a thin paper finish), and laminates such as formica, Wilsonart, and Nevamar. For longevity and ease of maintenance I generally recommend 4" on center grooves with a metal channel insert and laminate finish. It's a little more expensive than some of the other types, but it provides the best overall value for the cost. Metal channel is recommended when you need strength and durability for displaying your products. Metal channel is not easily damaged and retains its look for a much longer period of time. If you are on a tight budget, I recommend you consider spending a few extra dollars and purchase mealtime instead of paint grade slatwall. You won't be saving money by attempting to finish it yourself when you consider the additional cost of paint, brushes, rollers, primer, your time, and other supplies that may be needed. Slatwall has also proven to be a very versatile merchandising tool. I have seen it used successfully in most retail store environments. Slatwall can also be used as a decorative feature in your store. For example, by just changing the size of the channel from 4" to 6" or 12" on center you change the appearance but not the function of the unit. You can also create focal points in your store by using 6" or 8" on center channels to break the monotony of 4" channels on your walls. You might also consider putting colored laminate or vinyl strips in the channels to add a sense of excitement to your store's decor package. For clothing stores, slatwall can also be adapted to create focal points around a fitting room. Slatwall can also be used very effectively in bookstores, dinnerware outlet stores, pet stores, motorcycle stores, and sporting goods stores.

2. *Gondolas.* The gondola is a long, flat-bottomed, two-sided unit used to merchandise your products. *(See Photos 1.4, 1.5, 1.10, 1.35)* This fixture is most often designed with adjustable shelves combined with a flat, table-top surface with storage cabinet or shelve space below. The gondola is one of the most flexible store fixtures available to the retailer. The gondola has become a very effective merchandising tool for a variety of retail stores including automotive, health food, pet, hardware, bed & bath, motorcycle, bookstore, etc. The gondola is available in various heights, depths, lengths, and finishes depending on your budget, products, and needs. The gondola is frequently used in groups on the selling floor and positioned perpendicular to the main traffic aisles.

3. *Garment Fixtures.* Garment fixtures (or racks) are most often used to display clothing or other garments you feature for sale in your store. *(See Photo 1.9)* Garment fixtures vary in shape, style, finish, quality, and price depending on your particular need and budget. These store fixtures should be selected only after a careful evaluation of your specific needs is completed. Garment fixtures should be suited to the particular types of clothing or garments you sell and should fit in with the overall decor and image of your store.

4. *Glass Cubes.* Glass cubes are a universally used store fixture for most retailers. *(See Photo 1.15)* Glass cubes not only offer the retailer a great deal of flexibility, they are attractive and serve to enhance the overall image of your store. I have used glass cubes very successfully in recent years in the design of motorcycle and powersport stores. Glass cubes can be used to effectively store and display a wide variety of product lines - from motorcycle helmets to clothing to specialty items. You should, however, think through your specific goal for using glass cubes. Folded merchandise may look good displayed in glass cubes, but they become very labor intensive when employees have to continuously

re-fold and replace the merchandise after customers have removed it from the cube or put the item back in the wrong cube. Glass cubes do offer your customers an open view of your products helping to create subtle, yet effective, buying signals.

5. *Glass Showcases and Glass Towers.* Glass showcases and towers are larger examples of the glass cube. *(See Photo 1.16)* Glass showcases are used by many retailers as a base for their cash registers and wrapping areas. However, glass showcases used in this manner quite often end up becoming glass coffins filled with dead merchandise that gathers dust and is completely ignored by your customers. Why? Because the merchandise placed in these glass coffins is usually very difficult to get to by the customer. As a result, customers will frequently bypass the items in the showcases and move on to other products more easily accessible. Remember - a product that cannot be easily seen and easily handled by the customer becomes a product seldom purchased by the customer. Few customers want to wait in line to get to the register and then have to ask the clerk to see some item on the bottom shelf of the showcase while a half dozen angry customers are also waiting in line to pay for their merchandise. Customers interested in an item in the showcase will quickly become frustrated if they have to wait in line to ask permission to see a product.

A better alternative to the glass showcase might be the glass tower. The tower will usually take up much less space than the showcase and will be much more effective in displaying and merchandising your products. You will generally be able to fit three glass towers in the same space occupied by a glass showcase. Showcases are effective fixtures for displaying certain types of merchandise such as jewelry or more expensive products that usually require some type of employee assistance. For most other products, the glass tower will be a better choice.

6. *Four-Way Fixtures.* Four-way fixture units permit you to display merchandise from four different angles. *(See Photo 1.6)* In most cases, each arm is turned out at right angles from the center of the unit. This type of unit permits your merchandise to be displayed in a "face-out" or "front-facing" manner. The potential customer will be able to see the front of the first item on each arm of the unit. The arms that extend out from the unit are usually individually adjustable, up or down, so that the merchandise can be viewed from four different levels or angles. A variation of the standard four-way features arms that are waterfalled. This means that customers can see not only the entire front of the first item, but can also see the upper part of the following items in ascending order. The four-way unit is especially suited for displaying separates or coordinate fashions. For example, on one fixture it is possible to display jackets, coordinated slacks, blouses, and skirts that make up an ensemble outfit. The units can also be used to display coordinated color schemes. Four-way fixtures have proven to be versatile, flexible, and effective merchandising tools for many types of retailing operations.

7. *Wire Baskets.* Wire baskets have a multitude of uses in retailing. They come in a wide variety of sizes, colors, shapes, styles, and prices. They have become very popular fixtures for displaying smaller merchandise items that invite quantity purchases. They offer flexibility and can be easily moved from one location in the store to another. They are especially popular in discount or "99 cent" stores. Wire

baskets are especially effective when displaying items that are being featured as "Sale Specials" in your store. Perhaps you have ordered a large quantity of a particular item in order to receive a substantial price discount. Those items can be featured as a special sale and displayed in wire baskets throughout the store. The potential uses for wire baskets will be limited only by your imagination or creativity.

8. *Display Platforms and Pedestal Risers. (See Photos 1.15, 1.20, 1.21)* Platforms and risers are examples of "fluff" fixture components that can enhance your store's decor package and merchandising opportunities. Platforms and risers can help highlight products both large (motorcycles and watercraft) and small (helmets and gloves). You can further enhance the effectiveness of platforms and risers by using track lighting to draw attention to the product on display. Platforms and risers come in a wide variety of sizes and styles. They can be used in display windows, at the cash and wrap counter, and on the floor of your store. Since platforms and risers are so flexible, they can be used quite effectively to fill in those small island areas created in the loop traffic pattern. Platforms and risers can also be used to break up the monotony of your interior by elevating certain products for greater and more dramatic customer visibility (helmets or motorcycles, for example). Platforms and risers should be designed so that they complement your store's interior decor and image. *(See Photo 1.22)*

9. *Mannequins.* Like the familiar commercial slogan "You've come a long way, baby", mannequins have come a long way over the last twenty-five years. Contemporary mannequins are among the most effective fixtures available to the retailer today. Mannequins come in a wide variety of styles, sizes and colors. You can buy mannequins that are so life-like you have to look twice to distinguish them from a real live human being. Today's mannequins can be used in a multitude of retail settings to effectively and imaginatively display your products and merchandise. They can be used in conjunction with risers and platforms, gondolas, and other types of store fixtures. One of the most flexible type of mannequins available is the soft, full-body mannequin. It can be shaped and formed to fit the types of products you sell. *(See Photos 1.18 & 1.19)* At a recent trade show for the motorcycle and powersport industry, my staff and I constructed a 2400 square foot model store that included the use of six full-size mannequins completely dressed in full cycle clothing and gear. We received hundreds of comments from those visiting the store about the quality of the mannequins and their effectiveness in displaying our products and merchandise. Mannequins work! The soft mannequin is quite effective in creating a sense of action and drama when designing a window or in-store display. If you sell a lot of sport shirts or t-shirts, you could consider using the half-body Styrofoam mannequin. This type of mannequin helps give your product dimension and depth. It places your product in a real-life context. Mannequins should be changed and rotated on a regular basis to be most effective. Particular attention should also be paid to the care and maintenance of your mannequins. Nothing will detract more quickly from an effective display than using a mannequin that has broken or missing body parts. Mannequins, like every other store fixture, have one primary function: to help you sell more products! Well-dressed, well cared-for mannequins will help create an exciting buying environment in your in your store. Mannequins help your customers visualize how the product can look on them. So take

good care of them. Full-body mannequins are relatively inexpensive and can become one of your most effective merchandising tools.

CONCLUSION.

As I stated at the beginning of the chapter, my goal was to provide you with a basic overview of the types and styles of fixtures available to retailers today. The list provided was not meant to be complete nor comprehensive. It's a place to begin. Successful stores of today are those that set their sights on the future. Successful stores change as customer's needs and shopping habits change. Your fixtures tell customers a lot about your store. Make sure you purchase the right fixture for your products and merchandise. Buy the best possible fixtures you can afford. They are an investment in your store's continued success. If unsure of what fixtures you need, do not hesitate to contact a professional store planner to assist you. Selecting the right fixtures and arranging them in the right places in your store will help you increase your store's sales, increase your store's profits, and enhance your store's image. *(See Illustration on next page.)*

4 WAY DISPLAYER

METAL GONDOLAS WITH SOLID, PUNCH AND GROOVE, PEG BOARD BACKS

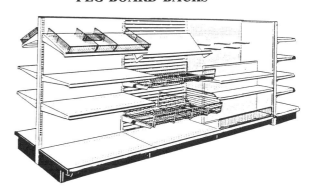

Panel Composition
• 3/4" Medium Density Fiberboard (MDF)
  (Veneer core optional)

T-Slat® Groove
• Easier to insert acessories
• Aesthetically pleasing

Metal/Vinyl Insert
• Increases strength
• Decorative Effect

SLATWALL

4 WAY GARMENT RACK

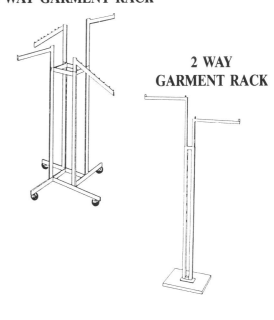

2 WAY GARMENT RACK

MERCHANDISING ACCESSORIES

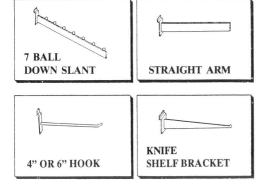

7 BALL DOWN SLANT

STRAIGHT ARM

4" OR 6" HOOK

KNIFE SHELF BRACKET

Note many of the basic store fixtures available to retailers of all sizes today. Most offer flexibility, adaptability, and are price competitive.

CHAPTER 8

HOW TO MERCHANDISE YOUR STORE LIKE THE PROS

"The effective merchandising of your products will do more to increase your sales than any other single thing a retailer can do!"
—Jim Rasmus, Professional Store Designer/Planner

INTRODUCTION

You've decided you want to open your own retail store. You find the right location; you secure all the financing to start your business; you construct the building (or you move into an existing building); you have a professional store planner assist with the design of your store; you order the fixtures and set them up; you order your merchandise and eagerly await its arrival. But now you start to wonder: "What do I do when all my merchandise arrives? What's the best way to arrange it on my fixtures in order to maximize my selling opportunities?" You've just described the essence of retail store merchandising. Merchandising is a term that describes the *promotion of merchandise sales, by coordinating production and marketing, and by developing advertising, display and sales strategies.* This chapter will focus on developing merchandising strategies that will help you to more effectively display your products, sell more merchandise, enhance your store's image, and increase your profits.

THE FIRST STEP

Effective merchandising is both a science and an art. To effectively merchandise your products you must understand something about the psychology of buying, your customers, the products you sell, and how those products should be displayed in your store. Effective merchandising involves bringing together all of the strategies we have discussed up to this point in the book. You should have already developed your business plan; you should have developed a strong working relationship with a professional store planner; you should have completed a comprehensive store walk-through analysis and evaluation; you should have implemented a workable traffic flow pattern in your store; and you should have updated and upgraded your fixture systems. You are now ready to begin the task of merchandising your products.

There are basically two options available to you. You can try to merchandise the products yourself. Or you can work with a merchandising specialist. A professional store merchandiser specializes in developing effective merchandising strategies for retail store owners. *(See Photo 1.23)* This individual will visit your store, analyze and evaluate your products, fixtures, and existing sales strategies, and make specific recommendations on how to arrange and display your products to maximize sales. As the owner or manager, you must determine whether you have the skill, insight, knowledge, and the time to develop an effective merchandising plan for your store. For most store owners, the best option is to work with your store planner to develop an effective merchandising plan, or to let your store planner recommend the services of a professional store merchandiser. Working with a specialist will free you up to take care of the day-to-day tasks that require so much of your time and efforts. The decision to do it yourself or secure the services of a merchandising specialist rests with you. The remainder of this chapter will develop some merchandising strategies that you can use if you choose to do it yourself.

EVERY DAY IS GRAND OPENING DAY!

I have completed hundreds of store walk-throughs and evaluations over the last ten years. In over 90% of those stores I visited one factor was immediately apparent: the store owners lacked even the most basic understanding of effective merchandising techniques. Yet, these same store owners were making all the decisions about how their products were going to be displayed. The results were usually disastrous: the wrong products on the wrong fixtures; using inappropriate fixtures to display products; ineffective use of display space; poor (or no) traffic flow patterns; clutter, congestion, and chaos; and, most importantly, lost sales opportunities. Successful merchandising involves much more than just putting products on a shelf or peg hook or in a bin. For your customers, successful merchandising should be more than "if you can find it, you can buy it." Yet, sadly, this attitude is present in far too many stores today. *(See Photos 1.4, 1.6, 1.7, 1.8, 1.10, 1.21)*

Successful merchandising is a skill that can be learned; but even more importantly, successful merchandising is an attitude that must begin with you - the owner. You must begin with the attitude that every day is Grand Opening Day in your store. Consider your Grand Opening day. It was probably one of the most exciting days in the history of your store. Your store was new; your products were new; you advertised and promoted the day; your store was neat, well organized, and well stocked with products; your staff and employees were eagerly anticipating the arrival of your customers; in short, you did everything possible to make the opening of your store a successful event. I'm convinced that many retailers continue to fail and go out of business because they have lost that "Opening Day" sense of excitement and they have allowed their stores to deteriorate in appearance, attitude, and commitment to customer service. You can change that. Begin with a commitment to make every day in your store a Grand Opening day! A successful and effective merchandising plan begins with the attitude you possess and communicate to your employees. The next step is to develop a comprehensive merchandising plan for your store.

SUCCESSFUL MERCHANDISING BEGINS WITH A PLAN

Merchandising your products successfully begins by developing a comprehensive Merchandising Calendar for your store. The Merchandising Calendar will help you in organizing your product displays and in keeping your merchandise turning over as quickly as possible. The calendar will help you to more effectively schedule all the special marketing and sales promotion campaigns. In addition, the calendar will tell you when it is time to put up and take down your displays. This results in a store that continues to look fresh and new and exciting - in short, as if every day was a grand opening day.

The Merchandising Calendar should be developed in accordance with your selling year. For some stores, the selling year may begin on January 1st; for others it may begin on October 1st, in anticipation of the Christmas season. Determine when your selling year begins and make that date the starting point of your Merchandising Calendar. Once this date is determined, you will want to involve your merchants and buyers (if you are large enough to have buyers on your staff) in the development of your Calendar. These individuals will assist you in determining when to buy merchandise, when to schedule seasonal or holiday promotions, and when to schedule annual selling events. You may also want to involve other members of your management team and sales staff in the development of your Merchandising Calendar. Planning for the annual Merchandising Calendar of events should begin two to three months prior to the start of your selling year. For example, if you operate on a calendar year basis, your selling year will begin on January 1st. Therefore, you should begin your planning in October or early November. You should build into the calendar the flexibility to switch or change events or promotions if the need arises. Remember, your objective is to plan in advance your sales and promotion campaigns in order to maximize sales opportunities throughout the year. Planning your merchandising events in advance will make it much easier to schedule your advertising for those events. You'll know when to schedule your newspaper advertising, direct mail campaign, TV and radio advertising, or any other advertising or promotion efforts you choose to use. A sample merchandising calendar, based on a January to December selling year, is included below.

SAMPLE MERCHANDISING CALENDAR (JANUARY TO DECEMBER)

JANUARY
Sales Events:
1. Post-Christmas and holiday
2. Pre-inventory
3. Furniture
4. Whites, foundations and lingerie
Special Promotions:
1. Bridal previews
2. Pre-Valentine's and President's Day
3. Travel and cruise
Tie-In Events:
1. Football - Bowl games and Super Bowl
2. Martin Luther King Day

FEBRUARY
Sales Events:
1. President's Day sales
2. Final winter clearances
3. Housewares
4. Pre-Spring sales
Special Promotions:
1. Valentine's Day
2. Spring fashions
3. Outdoor sports and recreation preview
Tie-In Events:
1. President's Day
2. Lincoln's and Washington's birthdays
3. Groundhog's Day

MARCH
Sales Events:
1. Pre-Easter
2. China, glass, housewares
Special Promotions:
1. Home and garden
2. Spring and Easter
3. New fashions and accessories
Tie-In Events:
1. St. Patrick's Day

APRIL
Sales Events:
1. Post-Easter
2. Pre-Summer
Special Promotions:
1. Easter
2. Summer wear, swimwear
3. Pre-Mother's Day
Tie-In Events:
1. Easter
2. April Fool's Day

MAY
Sales Events:
1. Memorial Day Sales
2. Baby Week
3. Spring clearances
Special Promotions:
1. Mother's Day
2. Bridal
3. Luggage/vacations
4. Summer sports and recreation wear
5. Outdoor living
Tie-In Events:
1. Mother's Day
2. Memorial Day

JUNE
Sales Events:
1. Furniture
2. Home furnishings

Special Promotions:
1. Father's Day
2. Graduation
3. Weddings
4. Summer wear/swimming wear
5. Camping
6. Sporting goods and recreational activities - biking, running, walking, tennis, cycling
7. Men's wear and furnishings

Tie-In Events:
1. Father's Day
2. Flag Day

This sample calendar illustrates how pre-planning can ensure greater success in the merchandising and promotion of your products. The key is to develop a calendar that reflects the sales events, special promotions, and tie-in events that are unique to your industry, products, location, and community. Developing a Merchandising Calendar of events will help you to maximize every opportunity to increase your sales throughout the entire year. The time you spend in developing an effective and comprehensive calendar will be one of the best investments you can make in your store and its continued success. We will now focus on seven specific merchandising techniques that you can develop and implement in your store today.

7 TECHNIQUES FOR EFFECTIVE MERCHANDISING

One of the primary objectives of effective merchandising is to create as many impulse sales opportunities as possible in your store. The following seven proven merchandising techniques will help you accomplish this important objective. These techniques are designed so that all your employees can be involved - on a daily basis - in the task of effectively merchandising your products. Expect no less from them.

1. *Front Face Products Daily. (See Photo 1.23)* Front facing simply means making sure that products are moved to the front of all your fixture systems at all times. For example, if you display items on peg hooks, and a customer purchases the first item on the peg hook, your sales associate should immediately bring the remaining items on that peg hook to the front. This ensures that your store always has a "full" product look. This technique helps eliminates the feeling that your shelves are low on products. Front facing gives the customer a sense of fullness in your store - even when you may be running low on certain products. When customers look at your shelves, they will see products on every hook or shelf with no gaps or empty slots. Make sure your staff or employees are instructed on the

importance of front facing merchandise at all times. By doing this on a regular basis throughout the day, your employees will be aware of the need to replenish from inventory any product that is running low on your shelves. This technique will enable you to know at all times what products are selling well, and what products are not.

2. *Spread to Fill. (See Photo 1.24)* Spread-to-fill does not refer to loosening your slacks after a big meal to make room for dessert. Spread-to-fill is a retail merchandising technique that helps you create the impression that your store is always product"full". To accomplish this, you simply take your extra merchandise on a shelf or hook or your face outs and spread them out to fill in empty shelves or hooks that may exist because a particular product is temporarily sold out. Again, your objective is create the impression that your store has ample products at all times on all of your shelves, hooks, or displays. Make sure you do not let your jobber or supplier talk you into letting your shelf or hook remain empty until the next order arrives- your job is to make sure every display fixture has a full product look. After all, if customers see too many empty or partially empty shelves, they will soon get the feeling that your store doesn't have the products they want - and they will shop somewhere else. Always spread-to-fill and front face all products. Teach this technique to your employees and expect them to practice it anytime they are working on the sales floor.

3. *Color Block Your Merchandise. (See Photos 1.25 & 1.26)* Successful merchandising in the 90's and beyond will involve much more than simply throwing your products on a shelf, hook, or rack and hoping the customer can sort through it all and find what they are looking for. Successful and effective merchandising requires that you be aware of your customer's needs and shopping habits. It also means being creative and flexible when you display your products. Color blocking is a technique that can help you accomplish that goal. Color blocking is a technique that takes advantage of your product's packaging and color. Let's consider motor oils as an example. Assume for a moment that you own a motorcycle store that offers motor oils for sale to customers. There are many different types and grades of oil available. In my experience, most retailers will arrange oil containers horizontally on a shelf by weight or grade. This means you will have one row on a shelf, another row on a second shelf, and so on. The customer is forced to spend valuable shopping time looking at all the rows in order to find the right grade. This method of merchandising creates difficulties for the shopper. Consider an alternative approach. We are taught in this country to read from left to right. This is an ingrained habit and is carried over into the shopping environment. It might make better sense to stock the product so the choices available to the customer read from the left to the right. In this example, instead of having the oils arranged horizontally by rows on the shelves, you would arrange the display of the oil in vertical rows - by color of package and grade - so that the customer can now look across the top shelf and read from left to right to find the particular grade or weight desired, pick the appropriate can, and move on to the next purchase. This approach can also be used for arranging apparel as well. Arrange by color on the shelf or rack. Many times a customer will purchase a product simply because it is their favorite color - regardless of the price. Using color arrangement to your advantage will result in more impulse sales! Utilizing the color blocking technique

is a proven way to create more attractive product displays, capitalize on shopper's buying habits, and increase your impulse sales opportunities. Teach it to your employees and make sure they apply this successful merchandising technique to your product lines.

4. *Practice the Two-Finger Rule. (See Photo 1.35)* No, I'm not referring to the peace or victory sign! The two-finger rule refers to a technique that enables you to maximize the use of your vertical display space on shelves and other fixture systems. The two-finger rule states that your products are spaced so that the top of the product on a shelf comes within two figure widths of the next shelve. Your goal is to utilize as much vertical space as possible for the display of your products. You undoubtedly have heard the old saying that "time is money". Well, in the retailing industry an equally important truth is that "space is money". If you rent your retail store facility you probably pay for the space based on cost per square foot. It is important, then, that you do everything possible to maximize the use of all your available retail display space. The two-finger rule enables you to do just that. I have talked with dozens of retail store owners who complained that they just didn't have any more space available for their merchandise. Wrong! What many of these owners are failing to do is to take advantage of the existing retail store space they have - and I'm not only referring to fixtures with shelves, but to pegged shelving units and garment units as well. The key point to be made here is that you do not merchandise your products higher than the top of the shelving fixture you are using. This applies to your floor gondolas primarily, and not to your wall units. By keeping your products at or below the top of your fixture unit you will eliminate the "Manhattan sky-line" appearance - that uneven look created when one product is higher than another on your shelving units. The best way to implement the two-finger rule is to first remove everything from your fixtures. You should then determine what products should be placed back on the fixture. Place an item back on the shelf to the two-finger depth. It may get a little frustrating the first time through but you'll soon learn what looks best and how much product you can comfortably place on the unit. Make sure you keep larger products on the bottom, with smaller products next, and so on.

5. *End-Cap Merchandising.* End cap (or simply end displays) are displays typically set up at the end of aisles or gondolas to promote a specific product or categories of products. End cap displays should focus on one or two products, if related. The display can be anything from the product itseslf simply opened up—such as dog bones in wire baskets in a pet store or shampoo and rinse in wire baskets in a beauty salon. End cap promotion focuses on large quantities of products that you generally receive a special buy on or that you wish to heavily promote. The goal is to use the end cap display to set off the featured products from all the other products. I visited a store not too long ago in Santa Fe, New Mexico. While walking through the store I noticed a large end cap display that seemed to feature a number of products. On closer inspection, I counted at least 27 different products on the end cap display. I rounded up the manager and asked him why so many products were being displayed on this particular end cap unit. His response: "I want to tell my customers what we carry." Well, we stepped back a few aisles and proceeded to watch customers as they walked by the unit. Not one customer (during a period of about one hour) stopped to look at the display or to purchase a product. My

recommendation to the manager was to focus on one product or a few products if related by category. For example, in a motorcycle store you might feature oil and oil filters on an end cap display. Walk into your local grocery store and you will see some very effective uses of end cap displays at the end of most of their aisles. Properly constructed and merchandised end cap units will sell products. But more importantly, end cap displays can promote and expand customer impulse sales. Take some time to develop effective end cap displays for your products and then frequently rotate the products displayed. Make sure your store always has a feeling of excitement. Well designed end cap displays give your customers additional reasons to buy products they may not have intended to buy in the first place (impulse sales!).

6. *Tonnage, Seasonal, and Promotional Merchandising. (See Photo 1.36)* Tonnage is a retail term that refers to buying large quantities of an item and creating a special merchandising display unit from which to sell the product. Effective tonnage displays will require that you commit to buying large quantities of an item - baby strollers, film for cameras, footballs, pet food, or motorcycle helmets. The product will usually be displayed on an elevated platform in a high traffic area of your store. Always use a platform to display tonnage merchandise. You should never set your product on the floor. Putting the items on a platform tells your customer you care about the products you sell. You'll also reduce the number of items damaged due to customer accidents. Tonnage display flats are also very effective if placed at the front windows of a store, near the front entrance, or at major customer traffic areas throughout the store. This is especially important if you are in the initial stages of designing your store, or if you are contemplating redesigning an existing store facility. Like end cap displays, tonnage displays should focus on a specific product and be rotated frequently. When buying products at your next trade show or expo make sure you buy enough for all your tonnage display units - especially if you are planning for seasonal or promotional events scheduled on your Merchandising Calendar. Always keep a sufficient inventory of these special items to ensure you won't run out of product in the middle of a winning sales event. Also keep in mind that your sales staff will have to pay particular attention to these display units and keep them well stocked at all times - especially if you are having a successful sale. These types of displays help to put the customer into a buying mood and should become an important part of your merchandising plan.

7. *Signage.* Signage refers to all the signs that are used to promote your store, advertise your products, and display your prices. *(See Photos 1.36 & 1.37)* Effective signage techniques will help you sell more products. Effective signage will accomplish a number of important objectives: tell customers what they are buying; inform customers about the benefits of purchasing your products; and communicate to the customers the price of the product. Do not make or use handwritten or drawn signs using pens, pencils, or markers. They will always look tacky and "cheap" and should be avoided at all costs if possible. You want to communicate a look of professionalism to your customers at all times. One way of accomplishing this is to have your signs printed by a professional printer if possible. You might also purchase some signage kits offered by many full service office products companies or retail-oriented mail order catalogs. During my 20 years serving the retail industry I've

seen many systems for creating effective signs, but none has produced more professional looking results than the Impulse System unit offered by Insignia. The unit is about the size and weight of a typewriter. The Insignia sign maker will create instant professional looking signs in many sizes and colors, all ready for immediate use in your store. There is no waiting for ink to dry or mistakes to correct. *(See Photo 1.37a)* Professional signage should be used sparingly (to avoid "graphic pollution"), always be informative, and be easy to read by your customers. When possible, try to use sign holders for all your signs. There are metal or plastic holders available from a wide variety of manufacturers at reasonable prices. Keep the signs you do use simple and easy to read, and take them down immediately following any special sales or events.

8. *Clean and Neat.* The one thing that you can do every day to make your store as presentable as possible to your customers is perhaps the easiest and least expensive: keep your store neat and clean at all times. If your goal is to make every day a Grand Opening Day then this one task must be at the very top of your priority list. Make sure that before the first customer walks through your doors your store has been thoroughly cleaned, vacuumed, fluffed, filled with products, and inspected by you for any last minute details that may need attention. Many concerned store owners and managers have developed a comprehensive pre-opening checklist that must be completed before the doors open to the public. Whether you do it yourself or delegate the responsibility to a trusted member of your staff is not what's important - what's important is that the store be cleaned and prepared daily before your opening. If you have a large store operation, you may want to consider securing the services of a professional commercial cleaning and maintenance organization. If you do, make sure you do not fail to let them know what you expect - after all, it's your store. Every one of your employees must be taught the importance of keeping the store neat and clean during working hours. Stress the importance of continuously inspecting the store throughout the day for opportunities to keep things neat and clean. Lead by example on this point and you will soon communicate to every one of your employees just how important a clean, neat, well organized store is to you. Communicate your expectations to all associates and then hold them accountable for results. This task should be the responsibility of all your employees, even those who may not come in direct contact with your customers. If they're walking through the store and they see a piece of paper laying on the floor, they should bend over and pick it up. If they're walking from the parking lot to the store and they see debris, they should feel a sense of responsibility and pick it up. If shelves need additional product, then someone should fill the shelf first and then take care of discussing with you or the appropriate supervisor, whose responsibility it should have been. Keeping your store neat, clean, and presentable communicates an unmistakable message of pride and caring to all your customers and potential customers - and that's everyone's responsibility. Make some signs that say "Every day is Grand Opening Day!" and place them at strategic points throughout your store - points where every staff member and employee is reminded of what's important to you and to your customers.

Merchandising is both a science and an art. Some of the most effective merchandising techniques available to you involve nothing more than common sense. Others involve some study, learning, and application. Do not hesitate to work with your professional store planner or merchandiser to become familiar with the specific techniques that may benefit your store. It could be one of the wisest investments you will ever make in the future success of your store. Practice the techniques and principles contained in this chapter and you will experience more impulse sales and increasing revenues. You will also experience a contagious spirit of pride and loyalty in the hearts and minds of all your staff - and who can place a value on that?

PART THREE

MANAGING YOUR STORE FOR SUCCESS

"Management is the art of getting other people to do all the work."
—Anonymous (No One Will Take Credit)

CHAPTER 9

DEVELOPING A WINNING TEAM: HIRING, TRAINING, AND RETAINING QUALITY EMPLOYEES

"Among the chief worries of today's business owners is the large number of unemployed still on the payrolls."
—Unknown

INTRODUCTION

Winning retail stores recognize the importance of developing a strong team of dedicated, productive and customer-oriented employees. This chapter will focus on the hiring, training and retaining of a quality team of employees. As I stated in Part One of this book, possessing a positive, success-oriented attitude must begin with you - the owner or manager. Your attitude, your values, your commitments will in one way or another be reflected in the attitude, values and commitments of your employees. Success really does begin with you. Therefore, as you consider the human resource needs of your store, you must be very clear in communicating your expectations to every potential employee. Before you advertise to fill a position vacancy you must first have thought through your expectations for the position and for the person performing the duties of this position. Before you interview and hire your first employee, there are some preliminary tasks that you must complete.

BEFORE YOU HIRE

Prior to hiring any employee, you should give serious consideration to addressing the following tasks.

1. *Develop a realistic assessment of your staffing needs for the next six to twelve month period.* Carefully think through your anticipated manpower needs for the next year. Consider your present level of sales, anticipated growth in sales during this period, and your expected staffing requirements to meet your sales projections. Make sure your sales projections are realistic. Because retail sales tend to be seasonal you should determine how many full-time and how many part-time employees you may need during this period.

2. *Develop specific job descriptions for every position you anticipate filling.* Developing a job description will force you to think through the specific duties, responsibilities, standards and expectations for that position. When developing a job description, you should address the following: job title, full or part-time position, hours, compensation, benefits, specific duties to be performed, reporting supervisor or manager, how performance will be evaluated, frequency of performance evaluations, what constitutes acceptable job performance and what constitutes unacceptable job performance. Job descriptions should be written and made part of your Employee Handbook.

3. *Complete the preparation of your Employee Policies and Procedures Handbook.* In the next chapter we show you how to develop this handbook. All the important policies and procedures unique to your store should be included in this handbook. The handbook will become the basis for communicating your expectations, standards and requirements to all new employees.

Once you have determined your manpower needs for the next twelve month period, developed job descriptions for all positions, and completed the preparation of your Employee Policies and Procedures Handbook, you are now ready to begin the hiring process.

RECRUITING, INTERVIEWING AND HIRING NEW EMPLOYEES

The hiring process actually begins by developing a strategy for recruiting potential employees. The most frequently used source of advertising job openings is the newspaper classified section. Using the newspaper has both advantages and disadvantages. Some advantages include: generally low cost; reaches a wide reading audience; and creates the opportunity for an immediate response. Some disadvantages include: those responding may not possess the qualities you are looking for; display ads can be very expensive in larger metropolitan areas; some ads may generate a large response of unqualified applicants requiring a significant amount of screening time and effort. There may be some other alternatives available to you. One of the most effective sources for finding qualified candidates to interview may be your existing employees. Encourage employees to make recommendations of individuals they might know to fill staff openings. Your employees are already familiar with your store, its policies and procedures, and the opportunities for career growth; therefore, they may be your best source for recommending someone to fill an available position. Once you have a number of candidates you are interested in, the actual interview process begins.

Conducting successful employee interviews requires skill, patience, and time. The actual time involved in the interview process will be determined by a number of factors. They include: nature of the position - is it full or part-time?; skills and abilities required; educational requirements; training requirements. The important point to remember is this: schedule ample time to conduct a thorough interview. Determine if you are going to use one or multiple interviews to make a hiring decision. Develop an interview checklist that includes all the questions you feel are important in evaluating the candidates skills, abilities, education, and personal qualities. During the personal interview you should communicate to the candidate the specific qualities and skills you feel are essential for the position. Discuss your store's philosophy and Mission Statement with the candidate. Try to determine if the candidate will "fit in" with the other employees in a comfortable manner. Will the candidate be a team player and contribute in a positive way to achieving your goals and objectives? It is extremely important that you recruit, interview and hire individuals who will make your store a better place in which to shop and work. Recruit up to your standards, not down to theirs. Avoid the temptation to just hire another "warm body" to fill a position. You may end up paying a steep price for a long time if you compromise on your standards and expectations. That price is often measured in poor performance, bad or negative attitude, discipline problems, or having the person quit after a few days or weeks on the job. The result: you will have to start the recruiting, interviewing and hiring process all over again - and this means spending more time away from your other duties and responsibilities, as well as your other employees. Organizing and preparing for the recruiting and interviewing process will help ensure that you end up interviewing more quality candidates, effectively communicating your standards and expectations to those candidates, and hiring the best possible candidate for the position. Failure to organize and prepare up front will frequently result in wasted time interviewing and training, low or negative employee morale, and higher than necessary employee turnover. It pays to plan, prepare and organize your recruiting, interviewing and hiring efforts. Our attention will now shift to the training of new and existing employees.

EMPLOYEE TRAINING AND DEVELOPMENT

Once the candidate has been hired your next objective is to provide the best possible training and development program for the employee. We will focus on three areas: orientation, new employee training, and on-going employee training.

NEW EMPLOYEE ORIENTATION

Once you have hired someone to fill a position vacancy you should consider setting time aside to bring the candidate into the store for a new employee orientation session. When I hire someone I give them a copy of our Employee Policies and Procedures Handbook at the close of the hiring interview. I will then set a mutually convenient date and schedule the individual to attend a mandatory new employee orientation session. If you hire individuals on a continuous basis you may want to schedule the orientation sessions on a specific date or dates (perhaps every Monday from 8:00am to noon, or once a month on a day of the week and at an hour that will not interfere with the overall operation of your store). Prior to attending the orientation the new employee is asked to read the entire Handbook and to write down on a blank sheet of paper any questions or concerns that might come up as they read through the manual. The employee (or employees, if you are hiring more than one employee) are asked to bring the manual to the orientation session. The actual orientation session should generally last two to three hours, although I know of many stores who devote an entire day to the orientation session. The amount of time you devote to the orientation session will be determined by the scope of the material you want to cover during the meeting. A sample agenda is included below:

8:00am - 8:15am: Coffee and refreshments.
8:15am - 8:30am: Introduction of staff and new employees.
8:30am - 8:45am: Review of agenda.
8:45am - 9:30am: Complete hiring forms and related paperwork.
9:30am - 10:15am: Review of Policies and Procedures Manual.
10:15am - 10:30am: Break.
10:30am - 12:00pm: Review of Policies and Procedures Manual.
12:00pm - 12:30pm: Question and Answer Session.
12:30pm - 1:30pm: Group luncheon.
1:30pm: New employee to assigned department and meeting with supervisor.

If you are a larger store and you recruit and hire multiple employees on a regular basis, you might want to consider having a full day orientation session. One of the principle benefits of conducting an all-day orientation session is the opportunity it provides your new employees to get to know each other as well as the opportunity to get to meet and talk with the key members of your store's management team. The final form your orientation takes will be determined by your specific needs, restrictions and requirements. Next: New Employee Training.

NEW EMPLOYEE TRAINING

Employee training and development should be an on-going effort, occurring at all times in one form or another in your store. For new employees training is especially important. No one likes the feeling we experience when on the first day of a new job we arrive promptly at the appointed hour, are greeted by the supervisor and end up being told "Here's your department; here's your register; if you have any problems or questions, I'll be in my office." You're left like a helpless lamb just waiting for the arrival of all the hungry wolves. Yet all too often that's exactly how many store owners and managers "train" their employees. Is it any wonder that the retail industry has such a high turnover rate? Providing your new employees with a quality training program will require a commitment of time, effort and money. I'm convinced they deserve at least that much from you. Here are some important elements of any new employee training program.

1. *New employee training should begin immediately following the orientation session.* If you do not have a "formal" training department, you may want to have each new employee meet with their immediate supervisor following the orientation session. The supervisor should be prepared to acquaint the new employee with any specific policies or procedures that are unique to the department they are working in. This may take the form of an informal classroom session, or it may be conducted "on the job" if that is more appropriate. One larger department store I am familiar with brings all new employees into a formal three-day classroom setting for their initial training. No one is permitted to work on the sales floor until they satisfactorily complete the classroom assignments. This is standard policy for all new sales associates in this store. The important point is this: Your employees must feel - from day one - that you are genuinely concerned about their success. They must feel that you are making a commitment to their success by providing competent and comprehensive training - both in the classroom as well as on the sales floor (or in their assigned department). The initial training must be organized and professionally presented if it is to be successful. If this task is the responsibility of a sales supervisor, then you must ensure that the supervisor is adequately trained and prepared to conduct the new employee training (you must make a commitment to "training the trainer"). Every new employee must be made to feel that they are not being "thrown to the wolves" and that you will do whatever is necessary to train and equip them to carry out their duties and responsibilities in a professional, competent manner. Your training must begin immediately following the new employee orientation session.

2. *New employee training should include the demonstrated attainment of specific goals and objectives.* During the initial training period for your new employees, you should establish a list of specific tasks that they must not only learn, but also be able to demonstrate on the job. Perhaps you determine that after three days, every new sales associate should be able to satisfactorily operate the cash register. Now you must determine what "satisfactorily" means. List the specific procedures they should have learned on the register during the initial three day training period. At the end of the three day period, test them on their knowledge of the procedures and test them on their ability to demonstrate competency on the register by completing the assigned procedures. Successful new employee training

must include the development of clear, specific, attainable and measurable standards of performance. 3. *New employee training must include frequent and honest evaluation of progress.* In the beginning, you (or the immediate supervisor) should sit down with the new employee on a daily basis to review and evaluate progress. This evaluation can take several forms. It can be informal. The supervisor can meet with the new employee over coffee at a scheduled break, over lunch, or at any other mutually agreeable time. There should also be a more formal evaluation session scheduled at the end of the employee's first full week. This session should include a thorough discussion of all learning requirements up to that point. This evaluation session might include not only the immediate supervisor, but also you or the store manager, if appropriate. New employees should know exactly where they stand at the completion of this performance review session: they should be made aware of their strengths and their weaknesses. Any weakness or area of concern discussed in the evaluation session should also include a recommendation of specific steps necessary to convert the weakness into a strength, and a realistic timetable for demonstrating competency. The new employee should never be blindsided - practice open and honest communication with every employee at all times! Following the initial new employee training program, performance reviews should be completed on a regular basis as outlined in your Employee Policies and Procedures Handbook.

4. *New employee training should focus on building a winning team attitude.* As discussed in Chapter One, the importance of creating a work environment that fosters the development of a positive success attitude cannot be overemphasized. This quality is one that must be exhibited by the new employee's supervisor, as well as evidenced by all existing employees. The importance of sincerely possessing this quality should be reinforced repeatedly throughout the new employee orientation and training programs. In addition, the initial training for new employees should focus on the importance customer service in your store. The truly successful retail stores are those that have made a strong commitment to customer service concerns. The successful retail stores of the 90's and beyond will demonstrate that commitment by hiring and training a staff that believes in and practices strong customer service at all times. The initial new employee training period is the perfect opportunity for you and your management team to communicate your commitment to the importance of possessing and practicing a positive success attitude toward other employees and toward every customer.

ON-GOING EMPLOYEE TRAINING AND DEVELOPMENT

Your commitment to quality employee training and development does not end with the conclusion of your new employee training program - rather, it begins there. For you to successfully recruit and retain quality employees, you must demonstrate a solid commitment to on-going employee training and development opportunities. Quality employee training should include the following elements:

1. *Training should be continuous and consistent.* You should schedule regular training sessions for all your employees. The frequency of the sessions will be determined by the size of your staff, the nature of the training material to be covered, and the urgency of covering the material. Most small to

medium sized retail stores will conduct training sessions at least monthly, with some as frequently as weekly.

2. *Training sessions must be planned and the trainer prepared.* In order for training sessions to be successful, they must be planned in advance. The material to be covered must be relevant to the needs of your staff. All training should have as its objective making your employees more competent and better prepared to perform their duties and responsibilities. In addition, the individual conducting the session must be prepared. Nothing will destroy the credibility of your training program more quickly than an unprepared trainer.

3. *Training should always reinforce the most important goals of your store.* Use every training session to reinforce those things that are most important to the continued success of your store. Remind the employees of your store's Mission Statement, or your commitment to customer service, or to the importance of a positive attitude. Your training sessions provide you with a golden opportunity to continuously reinforce to every employee what's important to the current and future success of your store.

4. *Training sessions should include rewards and recognition.* Every training session should set aside some time to recognize and reward employees who have made significant or important contributions to the store. Perhaps you received a letter from a customer praising an employee for exceptional customer service. Read the letter out loud to all those attending the training session, personally congratulate the employee, and provide some type of reward to reinforce the positive contribution. The reward does not have to be extravagant or expensive. It can be a lunch or dinner for the employee and their spouse, it can be a plaque or certificate of recognition, it could be a half day off, or it could be a small cash gift. What really matters is the fact that you recognized and rewarded positive performance. This action on your part will serve to reinforce to all your employees that your commitment to exceptional performance goes beyond just words - outstanding performance is something you desire and is something you feel is worthy enough to reward. A word of caution - always make sure recognition is sincere and done in the presence of other employees when appropriate. Your training sessions can not only be used to increase and enhance the professional development of your employees, they can be used as important motivational opportunities as well.

5. *Training sessions should feature outside speakers.* Use your training sessions to feature an occasional outside speaker or resource person. This individual should address a topic or subject that might not normally be covered during your training sessions. An outside speaker will help keep your meetings fresh and exciting. When scheduling an outside speaker make sure you communicate clearly what you expect from them. Identify the topic to be covered, the time allotted to the presentation, the format of the training session, and any other consideration you feel is important. Also - always confirm the credentials of your speaker. Make sure the individual has conducted successful presentations in the past. Don't permit the individual to use your staff as guinea pigs.

RETAINING YOUR EMPLOYEES

As mentioned earlier, employee turnover in the retail industry is very high. Every time an employee quits or resigns it costs you considerable time and money to replace them. If you can reduce your employee turnover rate and retain quality employees, you can effectively increase your profits. How can you accomplish this?

1. *To retain quality employees, invest time up front in the recruiting and interview process.* Make sure you have clearly defined job descriptions for all positions you seek to fill. Develop a comprehensive interview checklist that includes the important questions that must be asked and discussed during the initial interview with the candidate. Establish your hiring standards and do not compromise them. Hire every employee up to your standards and expectations. Contact references whenever possible. In short, do everything possible at this stage of the hiring process to make sure you are considering the right candidate for the job. Time invested at this stage of the hiring process may save you a lot of grief, heartache, time and money later on. Keep in mind - you should always hire for long term results.

2. *To retain quality employees, provide them with a copy of your Employee Policies and Procedures Handbook.* If you don't have an Employee Policies and Procedures Handbook, then take time to prepare one. Defining your policies, procedures and operating philosophy tells every employee what's important to you and what you expect from them. The handbook is an excellent tool to effectively communicate important information in a professional manner to your employees.

3. *To retain quality employees, you must expect them to be quality employees.* Communicate your expectation at every level of the interview and hiring process.

4. *To retain quality employees, train them regularly and professionally.* When employees know you are sincere about their career growth and development they will be less likely to look around for other employment. Keep the grass green on your side of the fence and your employees will not want to leave. Provide quality training programs for all your staff on a regular basis.

5. *To retain quality employees, compensate them fairly.* Adopt an attitude that quality people are worth quality compensation. You do not have to pay your people based only on what other competitors pay their employees. Compensate your staff fairly and review performance on a regular basis. Invest in your employees and you will reap rewards far beyond what you might expect. Earn a reputation for paying your people fairly and you will never be at a loss for people to work for you.

6. *To retain quality employees, recognize and reward outstanding performance.* This should be done on a regular basis and in front of the employee's peers whenever possible and appropriate. Let them know you care by your actions and your words. When employees feel appreciated, they will be less likely to leave. Do your best to create a genuine and sincere feeling of "family" in your store.

CHAPTER 10

ESTABLISHING AN EMPLOYEE POLICIES AND PROCEDURES HANDBOOK

*"Anyone who thinks employees aren't important should try doing without them
for a period of two months."*
—A Frustrated Store Manager

INTRODUCTION

Most businesses are a lot like human beings: they start out small and have rather simple needs but over time they grow bigger and develop more complex both in their needs and demands. Most retail stores start out small. The owner many times does everything - open the store, sell the products, keep the books, sweep the floors, hire employees, write letters, make the coffee, and close the store. The owner/manager invests a lot of time, effort, and TLC in making sure the store becomes successful and profitable. And, hopefully, over time, it does. The store experiences growth - in sales, in profits, and in the need to hire new employees. Now, the owner is faced with the need to delegate duties and responsibilities, to define duties and responsibilities, and to establish policies and procedures for the new people being hired.

But unfortunately, most owners, because they are still busy wearing so many hats, put off establishing those policies and procedures ("I just don't have enough time. . ."). The result is a business that lacks organization, continuity, and a clearly defined sense of purpose and vision. A more serious consequence of not defining company policies and procedures may be the violation of certain federal and state employment laws. It becomes absolutely necessary that every store operation or business, no matter what your size, establish written company policies and procedures. The balance of this chapter will focus on how to establish a company policies and procedures manual (or Employee Handbook).

WHY YOU NEED AN EMPLOYEE HANDBOOK

As a business owner, you should make the creation of an employee policies and procedures manual one of your top managerial priorities. The purpose of the policies and procedures manual is to provide your employees with a comprehensive summary of your company's policies, principles, standards, expectations and procedures. The employee handbook is not a legal contract; it is a summary statement of what's important to you about your store and how it is operated. It does not represent a contractual commitment by your store concerning terms of employment. Your store reserves the right to act in accordance with what is in the best interest of your company and its employees and is free to change the policies, principles, and procedures described in your employee handbook at any time.

You need to establish an employee handbook for a number of reasons. Among them are the following:

1. *To Define Policies.* An employee handbook forces you as an owner to describe and define your policies, procedures, and principles. Rather than keeping everything you feel strongly about in your head, you must now take time and reduce those thoughts and feelings to words and put those words on paper.

2. *To Inform New Hires.* An employee handbook clearly establishes what is unique and important about your business or store. All potential employees will have available before hiring the information necessary to inform them about your store's personnel policies and procedures.

3. *To Establish Uniform Standards.* An employee handbook establishes continuity and conformity. Specific rules, regulations, and procedures are clearly spelled out and apply to everyone on an equal

basis. This protects you, the owner, from accusations of preferential treatment of one employee over another.

4. *To Serve As A Resource.* An employee handbook becomes a source for answering employee questions about your store's policies, procedures, and rules. This will save valuable time in having to repeatedly explain policies and procedures to employees.

5. *To Promote and Advance Teamwork.* An employee handbook fosters a feeling of mutual respect and cooperation among employees and the owner/management team. The handbook will reinforce the importance of team spirit and teamwork in the day-to-day operation of your store, especially among your staff and employees.

6. *To Maintain Compliance With Applicable Laws.* An employee handbook will force you to comply with the appropriate local, state, and federal employment and employee regulations and guidelines.

7. *To Facilitate Employee Orientation.* An employee handbook provides you with an excellent tool with which you can develop and conduct new employee orientation programs.

WHAT TO INCLUDE IN AN EMPLOYEE HANDBOOK

An employee handbook can include whatever information you feel is relevant and important to you, your employees, and to the operation of your store or business. The employee handbook is a document that describes the policies, principles, and procedures that makes your store unique; it should include all the information that is important to you. We have summarized below some of the information that may be contained in a comprehensive employee handbook

1. *Preliminary Information.* You should consider including a brief introductory statement outlining the reason and purpose for the handbook. In addition, it might be an appropriate place to include a "Welcome" message from you, the owner, to your new employees. Some stores/businesses have also included a brief history of the company from its founding to its current position in the marketplace. This section should also contain a statement from the owner summarizing your business philosophy or mission statement.

2. *Employment policies and procedures.* This section should contain a statement about the following issues that relate to your company's employment policies and procedures:

— Pre-employment testing or screening policies. This section should address your company policies or procedures regarding required pre-employment substance abuse screening and testing.
— Store image and importance of public relations.
— Use of telephones, faxes for business and personal use.
— How you will communicate with your employees.
— New employee probation period (If any).
— Performance appraisal procedures.
— Availability of employee personal records.
— Employee salary and wage evaluations.
— Promotion and transfer policy.

— Employee disciplinary procedures.
— Procedures for submitting resignations.
— Work disruption procedures (especially during periods of inclement weather or emergencies).
— Attendance policy.
— Employee dress code.
— Company smoking policy.
— Non-compete policy (if any) upon termination of employment.
— Employee lunch and break policies.

COMPANY RULES AND REGULATIONS

This section describes those offenses, which because of their seriousness and nature, may involve immediate and summary employee discipline. Some examples are given below. Careful consideration by you, the owner, must be given to defining those offenses that would be serious enough to require disciplinary action.

1. *Discussing confidential company matters with unauthorized individuals.*
2. *Theft, stealing company property.*
3. *Endangering the well-being of other employees or customers.*
4. *Chronic absenteeism or tardiness.*
5. *Carrying dangerous weapons on company property.*
6. *Selling or distributing controlled substances.*
7. *Violation of company dress code.*
8. *Falsification of company documents.*
9. *Criminal misconduct.*
10. *Falsification of information on employment application.*

This is a representative list of some of the types of offenses or violations that many employers deem of sufficient seriousness to warrant immediate employee discipline or termination. Again, as we have stated, this section must include those items that are relevant to your store or business, and must be applicable to all your employees without exception.

GRIEVANCE PROCEDURES

This section of the employee handbook will outline your company's procedures for filing a grievance. You must recognize that in almost every employee / employer relationship there will occur those times when disagreements arise. There must be policies and procedures in place that define how those differences will be resolved for the mutual benefit of the employee and the company. These policies and procedures for resolving grievances must be fair and applied equally to all employees. One of the main reasons for writing the policies and procedures down is to ensure equal and fair treatment for each employee.

1. *Financial / Payroll Policies.* One of the most important reasons people work is to receive fair and just compensation for their contributions to the success of the company. This section of your employee handbook will contain information about how and when employees will be paid. For example, you should list the frequency of your paydays (weekly, bi-weekly, monthly, etc.); the day of the week on which employees will receive their checks; how the checks will be distributed; how hourly and salaried employees will be paid; overtime policies; recording hours worked; employee expense reimbursement policies and procedures; payroll deductions; completing required payroll forms for the company and the IRS; and any other financial or payroll related matters important to your organization.

2. *Company benefits.* An important element in developing a strong and long-term relationship between employee and employer is the provision for a quality package of employee benefits. We also recognize that no employer should be forced to provide any benefits beyond their ability to afford such benefits. Your company, like most companies, will probably not be in a position to provide many employee benefits during the early stages of your growth. As growth and profitability increase, your ability to provide a more comprehensive program of employee benefits will grow. The important point is this: describe in the employee handbook your company's current policies regarding the provision of employee benefits. Do you provide any? If yes, what do you provide? How does an employee qualify for the benefits? Are the benefits available to the employee's family? Is there a cost to the employee or will the employer pay for the benefits? This is your opportunity to define and describe your company's benefit plan. We've listed some of types of benefits available to employers, depending on the type of store you have, its location, and the number of employees you have. We recommend that you consult with your financial planner or insurance specialist for a complete description of what may be applicable and available to you.

— Group health and life insurance.
— Group short and long-term disability insurance.
— Dental and vision benefits.
— Prescription drug plans.
— Profit sharing plans.
— Employee stock option plans (if applicable).
— Employee voluntary payroll deduction plans.
— Qualified employee pension plans (401K's, etc.).
— Vacation policy.
— Paid holidays.
— Paid sick leave policy.
— Personal leave policy.
— Military leave policy.
— Jury duty policy.
— Direct deposit of employee payroll checks.

— Funeral leave policy.
— Workers' Compensation, Social Security, and Unemployment Compensation guidelines.

As you can see, there is a wide range of employee benefits and plans available to you. Select those that are important to you and your employees, those that you can reasonably afford to provide, and those that enhance and strengthen the relationship between you (the employer) and the employee. Employee benefits are just that - a benefit to your employees. Benefits are typically provided to employees over and above their cash compensation. Adding an employee benefit program can result in a significant increase in you company's expenses. Your decision to provide additional benefits to your employees must always be balanced with your ability to afford them. We counsel to begin slowly and to add benefits as you can afford them.

MISCELLANEOUS SECTION

Other items you may want to include in your employee handbook are: (1) A section describing the fact that all employer provided fringe benefits are subject to changes and modifications as a result of federal or state statutes. This section of the handbook will describe how those changes will be communicated to the employee; (2) A description of any other employer/employee issues not described in previous sections; (3) A statement to be signed by every new employee indicating that they have no unanswered questions, that they understand and agree with the policies and procedures, that they will comply with the stated policies and procedures to the best of their ability, and that willful violation of the stated policies and procedures may be grounds for disciplinary action, including immediate termination of employment.

Many employers establish a new employee orientation session immediately prior to or following the formal start date of the employee. During this new employee orientation session, the employee handbook can be reviewed in detail, questions answered, and the statement of understanding signed. A copy of the manual is then given to the employee.

ESTABLISHING AN EMPLOYEE HANDBOOK

The RDA Publishing Group has developed a sample Employee Handbook containing more detailed examples of the items discussed above. A copy of the Employee Handbook may be purchased from RDA at 50% off the normal retail price of $79.95. For readers of this book, the sample Handbook can be purchased for $39.95. The sample Handbook may be used a guide in developing your own company handbook. The RDA Publishing Group sample Handbook can save you hundreds of hours and thousands of dollars in production and development costs. To order your copy, call 1-800-RDA-WINS.

CHAPTER 11

MANAGING YOUR FINANCES: STAYING IN CONTROL

"I expect to spend the rest of my life in the future, so I want to be reasonably sure what kind of future it is going to be. That is my reason for planning."
—Charles Kettering
Industrialist (1950)

INTRODUCTION

If you are like most people, you started your business for a lot of reasons - to be your own boss, to satisfy a life-long desire, to make a lot of money, or simply to build something that you can call your own. You work very hard to make your business successful and profitable. You put in long hours, you wear many hats, and you do everything from clean the floors to sell your products to keeping your books. In other words, you are involved in every aspect of your store operation because you have a vested interest in its success. It's the dream of every business owner to reach a level of success that will enable them to achieve financial independence. As your business grows and you begin to generate sufficient cash flow to pay your bills and provide for your personal and family financial needs, it becomes increasingly important that you manage this money as effectively as possible. This chapter will focus on developing winning financial strategies that will enable you to manage, save, invest, and protect the money you will work so hard to earn. We will reveal how you can discover and implement the strategies necessary to achieve personal financial success, stability and independence. To achieve the level of financial success you desire will require a firm and unwavering commitment to not only knowing and understanding the principles that we will discuss, but more importantly, to apply and implement them in your personal situation.

Although there are hundreds of books, newsletters, and articles you can read on the subject of personal finance, we intend to focus "like a laser beam" on 10 basic, yet essential, winning financial strategies that can help put you on the road to financial success and independence. Your goal is to stay in control of this— as well as every— part of your business.

WINNING FINANCIAL STRATEGY #1: START TODAY

You've heard the old proverb before, but it bears repeating: "People don't plan to fail, they fail to plan." Sound like a cliche? It is. And the reason is obvious— thousands of people every day are engaged in the fine art of achieving financial failure. I don't know of anyone who gets up in the morning, looks in the mirror and says, "Good morning, World! Today I'm going to make sure I take one more step toward financial failure!" Yet, when reaching age 55, 60, or 65 many of us suddenly realize the reality of retirement is here— it is not something that's "way off in the future" anymore. The fear is real because for many there is nothing waiting for them except some vague hope that just maybe Social Security might provide some sort of income, however small it may be.

Consider the following statistics provided by the U.S. Department of Labor. For every 100 people starting their careers, the following situation exists at age 65: 29 are dead; 13 have annual incomes under the poverty level; 55 have annual incomes under $31,000 (with the median income being $7,300); and only 3 have incomes over $31,000. In which category will you be at age 65?

It is a paradox that in the world's richest nation, so many people will work hard all their lives only to end up living at or near poverty when they retire. Achieving personal financial success and stability has become the exception rather than the rule for most Americans. Why? Because most of us never begin to think seriously about our financial future until it's too late. We work and spend, work and spend, for over 40 years or more and then wonder why we don't have anything when it's time to retire. Working hard to build a successful business is important. But it's equally important that you stay in control of your finances as you build your business.

The first, and most important, strategy in achieving financial success is to resolve today to do something about your situation. Do not rely on someone else or some government social program to do for you what you should be doing for yourself. Take personal responsibility for your own financial well-being starting today. You are accountable for your own actions, so resolve to do the following now:

— Resolve to stop procrastinating any longer... Remember, putting off until tomorrow decisions you should make today only reinforces the cycle of indecision and failure.
— Develop a financial plan that relies on your own efforts as much as possible.
— Be accountable for your own actions... you cannot pass the buck to anyone else.
— Practice self-discipline every day.
— Put your financial plan in writing (just as you did with your Business Success Plan).

Take the first step toward achieving control of your finances by resolving to start today to develop and implement your winning financial plan.

WINNING FINANCIAL STRATEGY #2: KNOW YOUR ENEMIES!

The road to financial success can be long and dangerous to your financial health. There will be roadblocks and obstacles you must overcome if you are to achieve your dreams, goals, and aspirations. Just as in your business you must know your competitors and what they are doing, so too must you know your financial enemies. There are five enemies (or roadblocks and obstacles) you must not overlook.

1. TIME. Each day you wait to start your plan is a day that is lost forever. You can never retrieve or buy it back. Time is a fixed commodity for every one of us. Therefore, it is imperative that no matter what has happened to you in the past, you must begin to make time your ally, not your enemy. The financial cost of waiting can be dramatic. Consider the story of twin brothers Jim and Jerry. At age 18, Jerry decides to start saving $2,000 a year in an IRA after graduating from school (he plans to start college in four years). Jerry saves $2,000 a year for four years and averages 8% return on his money. He quits saving after four years and starts college. He does not touch the $8,000 he has saved over the four years until he reaches age 65. Averaging 8% return over this period, Jerry will have $287,668 waiting for him at age 65.

Jim, on the other hand, decides to go to college after high school and to begin his family and career before starting to save. Jim starts to save $2,000 a year in his IRA at age 35 and saves that amount for the next 30 years. He also averages 8% return over this period. Jim contributes $62,000 to his IRA by age 65, at which point he will have a total of $266,427 waiting for him. Jerry has saved a total of $8,000 over a four year period, and yet will end up with $21,000 more than Jim who has saved $62,000 over a 30 year period. This situation dramatically illustrates the necessity of putting time to work for you. Every year you wait to begin saving increases the necessity of having to work longer and harder to accomplish your goals. Overcome this enemy by starting to save today.

2. INFLATION. Inflation can be a deadly enemy to your financial health. Your financial plan must take into consideration the devastating effects inflation can have on your ability to achieve financial success. You should include in your portfolio investments that will allow you to keep up with inflation rates. Otherwise your money will continue to lose its purchasing power. Investing $100 today at 3% interest with 3% inflation simply means you made a net return of 0% on your investment. This is one enemy you cannot overlook when implementing your winning financial plan.

3. DESIRE FOR A HIGHER STANDARD OF LIVING. Most people want to be able to "keep up with the Joneses." However, if you want to achieve financial control and independence, you must continuously be on guard against the natural tendency to spend more than you earn. Determine what your standard of living will be then discipline yourself to live within your financial means. If you don't, this enemy will emerge victorious.

4. DEBT. We have become a nation of debtors. The vast majority of Americans owe more than they have in savings. Getting a credit card in our society is one of the easiest things you can do. My sons started receiving offers from credit card companies to apply for "pre-approved" credit while freshmen in college! These credit card vultures wanted them to start developing a credit-mentality before they even graduated from college. This buy now, pay later habit is one that is not easy to break. The only way to defeat this enemy is to learn to say "NO!" to the temptation to charge anything beyond that which you are able to pay off each month. Develop a resolve to pay off all existing consumer debt as soon as possible. Save the interest you are paying others and put it to work for you.

5. FINANCIAL IGNORANCE. One of the great tragedies of our day is the fact that so many individuals choose to remain ignorant about money and finances. They think that as long as they are working and making enough money to pay the bills, everything will somehow take care of itself. The only way to overcome this enemy is to discipline yourself to take charge of your financial situation— right now. Invest in some money management books, take a class on personal finance, or talk with a financial advisor you know and trust. Financial ignorance is not bliss—quite the contrary, it can become the surest way to financial failure there is.

WINNING FINANCIAL STRATEGY #3: PAY YOURSELF FIRST.

A 55 year old owner of a large powersports store came up to me after a workshop I was conducting at a trade show and expressed great concern that he could not afford to even think about retirement. For the past 18 years he never really worried about retirement because he was too busy building and running his business. The result was that he had not saved anything for his retirement, even though the last five years were the most financially successful in the history of the dealership. The problem: the owner never learned the strategy of paying himself first.

You may not be able to afford to set aside much for your financial goals when you start out, but those who do achieve financial success seem to have one thing in common— they developed the habit very early of saving something, no matter how small the amount, for their future. Remember this—*when you retire, it won't matter at all how much you earned; what will matter is how much you saved.* Your most important asset is not your store or your products or even your customers. Your most important asset is your ability to get up every morning, go to your store, and earn a living. The most important financial habit you can ever develop is the habit of paying yourself first. Learn to set aside something on a consistent and regular basis for your long-term financial needs and goals. You should strive to put at least 5 to 10 percent of your income into a special account to be used for your future needs. Pay yourself first—if you don't, no one else will.

WINNING FINANCIAL STRATEGY #4: TAKE FINANCIAL INVENTORY

Most retail store owners set some time aside on a regular basis to take inventory. It is an important part of managing your business. In like manner, it is critically important for you to set aside some time to take financial inventory on a regular and consistent basis. If you are sincerely committed to the goal of achieving financial control and independence, it is absolutely imperative that you take time right now to conduct a thorough and comprehensive personal financial inventory. Before you start you will need to gather some important information and documents. Included should be the following: (1) recent paycheck stubs or income statements; (2) tax returns (2 years); (3) record of personal expenses for last year, including cancelled checks, receipts, etc.; (4) all consumer credit card debt records; (5) bank saving and checking account statements; (6) investment records or statements; (7) insurance policies; (8) employer benefit statements; (9) mortgage information; (10) will and estate planning documents, if applicable; (11) any other financial information you feel is important. Now you are ready to complete your Personal Financial Inventory.

1. ORGANIZE YOUR RECORDS. The first step is to organize your records. Your financial documents and records should be placed in file folders or in a large accordion file. Some documents, such as a copy of your will, should also be placed in a more secure location. *Illustration 11.1* at the end of this chapter describes where some of your important documents should be located and how long they should be kept.

2. COMPLETE A NET WORTH STATEMENT. Next you will want to complete a net worth statement. This statement serves as a snapshot, or picture, of your financial situation at a particular point in time. The net worth statement compares what you own (your assets) with what you owe (your liabilities). On one side of the statement you will list all your assets and the appropriate dollar amount. On the other side of the statement you will list all your liabilities and the appropriate dollar amount. Total the assets and the liabilities. Subtract total liabilities from total assets and you have arrived at your "net worth." Your net worth should be a positive number and should be increasing each year. If your liabilities are greater than your assets you may be in financial trouble. You will need to devote some time and effort to reducing your debt load. You should prepare a net worth statement twice a year to start and then at least annually. We have included a sample net worth statement at the end of this chapter for your review *(see Illustration 11.2).*

WINNING FINANCIAL STRATEGY #5:
DEVELOP A PERSONAL OR FAMILY BUDGET.

Every successful business prepares a budget that reflects anticipated income and expenses. The budget is a planning tool that enables the business owner to make sound and informed financial decisions. Without a detailed and comprehensive budget a business would literally be operating in the dark without direction, purpose, or goals. If a budget is so important to businesses, then why isn't it equally important to individuals and families? The answer should not surprise you—most individuals do not have a personal budget because they do not know how to prepare one and because they don't have the required discipline to live within a budget if they do have one. A properly developed personal or family budget is absolutely essential if you are to gain control of your finances. A budget will serve as your guide and will help you manage your money more effectively. A budget will help bring a sense of order, discipline, and accountability to your efforts. Once you have organized your financial records and completed a net worth statement you are ready to prepare your budget. Here are some guidelines that may help you with this task.

1. COMPLETE YOUR NET WORTH STATEMENT (see Winning Strategy #4).

2. ESTABLISH A WRITTEN SUMMARY OF YOUR IMPORTANT FINANCIAL GOALS. You must decide what your most important short term and long term financial goals are and write them down. Do you want to be out of debt? Do you want to have a down payment for the purchase of a new home? Do you want to save for retirement? Do you want to save for your children's college education? Whatever your personal goals are, list them on a sheet of paper. Then you will want to establish some priorities. List each goal in the order of importance to you. Then decide when you want to accomplish that goal and write the date beside the goal. This summary will serve as a guide for you. It is very important that you know what your financial goals are and the most effective way of accomplishing that task is to write them down.

3. PREPARE A MONTHLY INCOME AND EXPENSE STATEMENT. An income and expense statement reflects your anticipated income and a summary of your projected expenses for a specific period of time (monthly, for example). On a sheet of paper list all sources of income for you and your spouse. List both gross income (before taxes and deductions) and net pay (your "take home" pay, after taxes and deductions). Your take home pay is important because this figure reflects the actual amount of money you will have to pay bills and to invest. Add to this any other sources of income you have (such as rental income, interest or dividend income, etc.). Calculate your total net monthly income from all sources and write that figure down. Next, list all your normal living expenses. Be sure to include those expenses that are not paid on a monthly basis (annual or semi-annual insurance premium payments, annual tax payments). Make sure you do not overlook any expenses. Include amounts for such things as lunches you buy at work, personal care items, pet food and supplies—any expenses that you might incur on a regular basis. Total these amounts and calculate them on a monthly basis. Total all your estimated monthly expenses (don't worry about being exact down to the penny—the important thing is to include all expenses, even if you have to estimate). Subtract your

monthly expenses from your monthly income. You may be in for a surprise if you have not done this before. Is the result positive (more income than expenses)? Or is the result negative (more expenses than income)? If expenses exceed income, then join the deficit spending club. You are living in exactly the same way that our federal government lives— by spending more than you earn. But unlike the government you cannot continue to spend more than you earn. It will catch up with you very quickly and the result can be disastrous. If your expenses are more than your income you have basically three options: (1) spend less; (2) earn more; (3) do both. You must determine what option is best for you. A sample Income and Expense Worksheet is included at the end of this chapter. *(See Illustration 11.3.)*

4. INVEST IN A BUDGET WORKBOOK. For under $20 you can purchase a comprehensive budget planning workbook from most office supply stores that includes many of the worksheets you will need to prepare your budget. It may be a wise investment to help you get started.

5. KEEP TRACK OF ALL YOUR EXPENDITURES. It is often very helpful to write down all your expenses for a period of time (a month or two, for example) as you get started in the budget preparation process. Purchase a small note pad and carry it with you for a month. Keep a written record of every expenditure you make during the course of a day, of a week, of a month. Before you go to bed at night, write down all your spending for the day. Save receipts from all purchases and record them in your notebook. The purpose of this exercise is to make you aware of just how much money you may be spending without realizing it. If you are to gain control of your finances you must know where and on what you are spending your money. This is especially important if your expenses are greater than your income. Discipline yourself to do this for at least a month and you may be quite surprised at the result.

6. BREAKING BAD HABITS. Developing a personal or family budget may be the easy part. The hard part of this process is to break any bad spending habits you may have identified. Your success depends on doing some things that may hurt a little now, but will pay great dividends in the future. For your efforts to succeed, consider doing the following: (1) destroy all credit cards and adopt a pay-as-you-go attitude; (2) set aside 5 to 10% of your net income each month in a separate savings account to be used for long-term saving and investing for your future; (3) pay by check for as many purchases as possible; (4) learn to live within your means—no matter what the pain. Remember, you're in this for the long haul. You will never experience the benefits and joys of financial success and independence unless you are willing to sacrifice and pay the price now. If you don't, you will pay a much greater price later on.

WINNING FINANCIAL STRATEGY #6:
ESTABLISH A FINANCIAL RESERVE FUND.

Most financial planners and advisors strongly recommend that you establish a personal or family financial reserve fund as part of your planning. The purpose of this fund is to provide cash for the payment of unexpected or unanticipated expenses. Perhaps the car will need a set of tires that you were not planning on. Or the washer breaks down and needs replaced. Whatever the unexpected event, this fund is designed to help you pay for those expenses without having to go into debt to do so.

Another purpose for this fund is plan in advance for any non-monthly expenses and to begin saving in advance so that when the bill does come you will have the necessary money available to pay it. A third purpose of this fund is to save in advance for any insurance deductibles that you may be responsible for. For example, you may have a health insurance plan that calls for you to be responsible for a $250 initial deductible. Saving in advance for this possibility will enable you to pay the deductible without having a financial crisis occur.

How large should this emergency receive fund be? Most experts recommend that you try to save an amount equal to at least three to six months take home pay. The actual size of the emergency fund will depend on the following factors:

First, stability of income. The more stable your income, the less you need in an emergency fund. For example, a seasonal construction worker or a commissioned sales person may need a larger emergency fund than a salaried employee. Also, a large amount of unearned income, such as interest or rental income, reduces your need for a large emergency fund. Second, degree of insurance coverage. You should analyze the risks covered under your health, property, and liability insurance. Your need for a large emergency reserve fund decreases as the quality and amount of insurance coverage increases. Third, amount of cash likely to be needed. Your regular monthly expenses will guide you to the total amount of cash you may need. Establish your reserve fund and leave it alone until you need it.

Where should this fund be kept? Your emergency reserve fund should consist of cash, or assets that can be converted into cash very quickly. Using a bank passbook savings account or money market fund for this fund is recommended. You want to have access to the funds when you need them without delay or without suffering a financial penalty. A passbook savings account is recommended because the funds can be easily transferred to your checking account when needed, usually by making a telephone call. Most money market funds provide check writing options that enable you to access the money in your account easily and quickly.

Each time you get paid, you should make regular deposits into this account until you reach your fund goal. When an expense does occur and you use some of the funds in the account, resume making contributions to the fund until the amount is replenished. Get into the habit of building your emergency fund up to the level appropriate to your needs.

WINNING FINANCIAL STRATEGY #7: KNOW YOUR RISKS AND INSURE THEM

Insurance planning is one of the most important components of your financial program. Failure to take the necessary time to adequately plan here could prove to be one of the costliest financial mistakes you will ever make. Here are some guidelines that will help you more effectively plan for your insurance needs.

1. FIND AN INSURANCE AGENT YOU TRUST. I realize this can be easier said than done. You should understand that there are different types of insurance agents you can work with. Captive agents represent one company and usually offer products and services from only that company. Independent

agents represent more than one company and generally try to shop your insurance needs around to find the best policy and premium. Financial planners are usually licensed to sell both insurance and investment products and have completed courses enabling them to become certified as a professional financial planner. Insurance agents that have completed advanced courses to earn certification may have one or more of the following designations: CLU (Chartered Life Underwriter); ChFC (Chartered Financial Consultant); CFP (Certified Financial Planner). When talking with an insurance agent or financial planner it is very important that you discuss how they are compensated. There are basically three ways an agent or planner may be compensated: (1) Fee only basis; (2) Commission only basis; (3) Combination fee and commission basis. Do not hesitate to interview several agents or planners until you find someone you feel comfortable working with. You should seek an agent or planner that is professionally trained, competent, properly licensed and has no record of outstanding complaints or violations with your state's insurance commission or securities department. Most importantly, find someone you trust.

2. DO NOT TRY TO INSURE EVERY RISK. Potentially severe losses should always be insured. When a potential loss is not likely to harm you financially, don't waste money insuring that risk. Bear the risk yourself. Property insurance deductibles use this principle. You "self insure" the potential loss up to the amount of your deductible. Losses over and above this amount are paid by the insurance company. The more you self insure, through a higher deductible, the cheaper your insurance premiums. You decide how much of the loss you are willing to assume and then set that amount aside in your emergency reserve fund. When a loss is incurred, you will have the necessary funds available to cover the deductible. This enables you to gain control of your finances and to manage your money more effectively.

3. INSURE YOUR MOST SERIOUS RISKS. The two greatest risks you face are: (1) The financial risk caused by the unexpected loss of your life; (2) The financial risk caused by unexpected disability due to accident or illness. Your ability to earn an income is your most valuable asset. Stop for a moment and consider how much money you may earn over your lifetime. If you earn $40,000 a year and you work for 40 years, you will earn $1.6 million! (*see Illustration 11.4*). These earnings could disappear completely, however, if you die or become totally or permanently disabled prior to retirement. You and your family need to plan and protect against these two potentially devastating financial risks.

4. LIFE INSURANCE PLANNING. At death your ability to earn an income and your ability to save for the future ends. While no one likes to think about death, failure to plan for this possibility could have a disastrous effect on your loved ones. Statistics show that one out of every five persons between the ages of 30 and 40 will die before reaching age 65. Providing adequate life insurance will help your family maintain financial stability during the most difficult period they will ever face. Life insurance will pay your family tax-free dollars to replace the income you would have earned during your lifetime. Without it, what will they do?

HOW MUCH INSURANCE SHOULD YOU HAVE? There is no simple answer to that question. The best approach is to sit down with your insurance agent or financial planner and complete a detailed needs analysis based on your current financial situation. A number of factors should be considered in determining the amount of life insurance you should have: current assets, current liabilities, college education needs, family income needs, mortgage, cash available, existing insurance policies in force, group life insurance, and your investments. We have provided a sample life insurance worksheet at the end of this chapter *(see Illustration 11.5).*

WHAT TYPE OF POLICY SHOULD YOU BUY? Again, there is no simple answer to this question. You have three general types of life insurance policies from which to choose: term, permanent (or whole life), or flexible policies (universal life, variable life). The type of policy you should have will be determined by the purpose of the life insurance, the amount of life insurance you need, your age, your health, premium affordability, and how long you may need the coverage to remain in force. Be cautious of any agent or financial planner who recommends you purchase only one type of life insurance policy (term or whole life, for example) regardless of your need. Some agents will only recommend permanent, or whole life, policies. Some agents will recommend only term policies. The right answer for you will be determined by your particular needs. A good agent will help you determine your needs and then recommend the type of policy that meets those needs. There is a place for each type of policy when planning someone's insurance needs.

SHOULD I CONSIDER BUYING LIFE INSURANCE THROUGH THE MAIL? Generally, the answer is no. Most of the policies sold through the mail or on television have higher premiums, restrictions that may not be readily disclosed in the advertisement, and some that are sold to senior citizens have reduced death benefits during the early years of the policy. You should try to work with your existing agent when considering the purchase of your life insurance. If you do not have an agent, interview some until you find one that you trust and feel comfortable working with. Not all life insurance agents are fast-talking, high pressure, pushy individuals. Most are competent, well-trained, concerned, and dedicated to helping you find the right policy at the right premium. Seek them out and stay away from mail order and television offers. If it sounds too good to be true, then it usually is.

5. DISABILITY INCOME INSURANCE PLANNING. Disability income insurance is an important part of your insurance program. The odds of suffering a long-term disability at all ages exceed the chances of death (Source: Social Security Administration). Disability insurance policies provide for the payment of a monthly benefit that will help you pay your bills and maintain your standard of living should you ever suffer a long-term disability due to sickness or accident. Your ability to earn an income is your most important asset. If you could not work for an extended period of time who would pay your bills? Your mortgage or rent? Your car payment? Who would save money for your retirement or your children's college education? Consider the following potential sources of income available to you during a period of disability:

—*Your salary*. Do you have a short-term disability income policy through your employer? What percentage of your income will it pay? For how long?

—*Your savings*. How much savings have you accumulated? How long would it last to pay your bills if you were disabled for three months or longer?

—*Borrowing*. Would you be able to borrow money to pay your bills if you became disabled? From whom could you borrow? Friends, relatives, family members? Would your bank loan you money if you could not work?

—*Sell your assets*. Do you have any assets that you could sell if you became disabled (property, automobiles, other assets)? How quickly could you sell those assets? Could you get a fair price if you were forced to sell in a hurry in order to raise cash to pay bills?

Unless you are independently wealthy, you should consider the purchase of a quality disability income policy to protect yourself and your family against the potential financial loss you would incur if a disability should strike. Make sure you discuss the following policy features with your agent when considering the purchase of a disability income policy:

—*Definition of disability*. This is the single most important provision in your policy. Some policies require a total disability in order to collect any benefit. More liberal policies define disability as the inability to perform the duties of your own occupation.

—*Is your policy renewable*? Some disability policies allow the insurance company to cancel the policy or to refuse renewal. Make sure your policy is guaranteed renewable and is non-cancelable.

—*What is excluded from the policy*? You want to purchase a policy that has the fewest possible exclusions.

—*When will you start to receive benefits*? Most companies require a waiting period of at least 30 days before benefit payments begin. You can extend that period of time to 60 or 90 or 180 days or longer and receive a substantial reduction in your premium (you are self-insuring for this period of time).

—*Are you protected against inflation*? In 20 years, 4% inflation will reduce the purchasing power of a $2,000 per month disability benefit to just $913. You should make sure your policy has an inflation adjustment clause to protect you against the effects of long-term inflation.

What about Social Security? I've encountered many individuals who tell me they don't need to purchase a personal disability income policy because they are covered by Social Security. What they don't know is that out of every 1000 people that file a claim with the Social Security Administration to receive disability income benefits, 691 are rejected. Of the 309 who do collect any benefits, many did so only after waiting many months (or years) for their claim to go through a lengthy four-step appeals process. In order to be classified as disabled by the Social Security Administration you must pass nine tests in order to meet their definition of disability. We have included a summary of those tests at the end of this chapter *(see Illustrations 11.6 and 11.7)*. If you are counting on Social Security to meet your disability income needs if something unexpected happens, you may be in for a rude awakening.

Protect your most valuable asset—your ability to earn an income and to save money—by purchasing a quality personal disability income replacement policy.

You will face a number of important financial risks when planning your personal finances. Make sure you know those risks and insure them. They include: (1) Life Insurance; (2) Disability Income Insurance; (3) Property Insurance; (4) Health Insurance; (5) Liability Insurance.

WINNING FINANCIAL STRATEGY #8:
INVEST FOR THE FUTURE

Not long ago I was in Arizona to speak to a group of national sales managers on the subject of "Investing For The Future." After the presentation a number of the participants came up to ask some questions about their own financial situation. Without exception, the most frequently asked question was this: "Why is it we didn't learn about these investment principles years ago?" Most of us spend 12 to 16 years developing skills to earn a living. The problem most of us face is not earning an adequate income; the problem is learning how to manage the money we will make during our lifetime. As we have stated earlier, when you choose to retire it does not matter how much money you have made; the only thing that will matter is how much of what you earned did you save. Here are some important guidelines that will help you successfully invest for your future.

1. INVESTING FOR THE FUTURE REQUIRES PREPARATION. Developing a winning investment strategy does not happen by accident. It requires careful planning, preparation, discipline, and commitment on your part. First, you must take financial inventory. This is your starting point. Any investment plan you develop must begin with where you are today. As we stated earlier in this chapter, taking financial inventory means: (1) setting your financial goals; (2) developing a personal or family budget; (3) preparing an annual net worth statement; (4) organizing your financial records. Second, you must pay off all consumer debt. A sound investment program must be built on a foundation free of consumer debt. Every credit card or charge card you are paying on means money not available to invest for your future. It also means you are paying interest to someone else instead of earning interest on your money. Paying off consumer debt can add substantial dollars to your budget for long-term saving and investing *(see Illustration 11. 8 for a sample Debt Summary Form)*. Third, learn to pay yourself first. As we have stated, if you do not pay yourself first, no one else will. This requires a firm act of personal discipline on your part. You should start today to set aside at least five to ten percent of your net income for long-term saving and investing purposes. Fourth, establish an emergency reserve fund. This fund should be highly liquid and be placed in an account that is easily accessible without financial penalty. Fifth, make sure you have in place an adequate life insurance and personal disability income insurance program.

2. BASIC PRINCIPLES OF INVESTING. Any winning investment strategy must focus on this one basic objective: *to earn the maximum possible rate of return on your investments, consistent with your investment objectives and the amount of money you have to invest.* Here are some principles that should guide you in developing a winning investment plan.

First, understand that there is no such thing as a "perfect investment." Everybody would like to find that one investment that offers all of the following: high yield, no risk, not taxed, highly liquid, no penalties, no paperwork, easily understood, and it's legal! All investments have certain characteristics and the wise investor should be familiar with them. When developing your investment program, you should focus on those investments that have the qualities that are important to you.

Second, you should become familiar with investment characteristics. *Liquidity*— describes the ease with which you can convert your investment immediately into cash. *Safety*—describes the ability of the investor to receive the full amount of the principal invested. *Total Return*—refers to the earnings received on your investments (interest, dividends, capital gains). *Tax Status*—describes the tax treatment of the investment itself or the interest earned on the investment principal.

Third, successful investing for the future will require time, effort, discipline, and commitment. To experience success with your investment program you will need to: (1) start today—do not procrastinate another day; (2) diversify your investments—do not place all your investment dollars in one basket; (3) exercise self-discipline—once you start your program, stay with it . . . remember you are investing for the long-term; (4) live within your means— learn to spend only what you have budgeted and do not practice deficit spending.

Fourth, examine your investment alternatives and select those that you are comfortable with. There are dozens of investment alternatives available to you and there are dozens of so-called investment "experts" who stand ready and willing to give you their advice and take your money. The only right investment for you is the one that will allow you to sleep well at night—regardless of what anyone else tells you! Among the saving and investment options available to you are: passbook saving accounts; money market funds; annuities; cash value life insurance policies; Certificates of Deposit (CDs); stocks and bonds; mutual funds; collectibles; and employer sponsored plans (IRAs, 401K plans, Simplified Employee Pension Plans; stock purchase plans).

Investing for your future will not be easy. It will require time, effort, diligence, and patience on your part. Begin today to take control of your financial situation and your future can indeed be a bright one.

WINNING FINANCIAL STRATEGY #9:
PLAN YOUR WILL AND ESTATE

Most of us will spend a lifetime working to accumulate our estate. That estate will include cash, investments, insurance proceeds, real estate, business assets, or government benefits. At death, we want to have our estate passed on to our loved ones as in tact as possible. Unfortunately, as much as 15 to 60% or more of our estate may not make it to our family and loved ones. Why? Taxes, expenses, probate costs, fees. Will and estate planning can greatly reduce the potential loss of your estate. Here are some guidelines that may help you plan your estate more effectively.

1. BUILD YOUR FINANCIAL PLANNING TEAM. Your team should include: your attorney; your life insurance agent or financial planner; your accountant or tax preparer; your investment advisor; your bank trust officer. These are the individuals that you will work with throughout your lifetime to

effectively develop and execute your financial plan and all of its component parts. These individuals will provide you with counsel, advice, and recommendations about the many decisions you will have to make regarding your personal financial plan. They should be people you believe in, trust, and have the highest regard for.

2. HAVE A WILL PREPARED—IMMEDIATELY. It does not matter how old you are, what your income is, or what your family situation is. You should select an attorney you trust and have a personal will prepared as soon as possible. If you are married, it is even more imperative that you do this. Your attorney will advise you if you should consider establishing any trust agreements. This will depend in large part on many factors, including dependents, size of estate, business considerations, health, and other factors as determined by your attorney. Your will and other legal documents should be reviewed periodically as recommended by your attorney.

3. PURPOSES OF ESTATE PLANNING. The estate planning process will address many needs and concerns. Among them are the following: (1) to assure financial security for you and your family during your lifetime; (2) to create certainty that your estate will be transferred after death according to your wishes; (3) to minimize taxes, expenses, and delays in connection with the transfer of your estate; (4) to provide estate liquidity; (5) to retain flexibility; (6) to promote peace of mind.

4. PROBLEMS WITHOUT AN ESTATE PLAN. Without a will or an estate plan in effect at death, a number of problems may be created. Among them are: (1) estate transfer problems at death; (2) possibility of paying unnecessary taxes; (3) possibility of additional legal fees and expenses; (4) possibility of estate transfer delays; (5) possibility of forced sale of estate assets to pay taxes and expenses; (6) the naming of guardians for your children. As you can see, the potential for serious problems exist without a properly drafted and executed will and estate plan.

5. WHO MAY NEED AN ESTATE PLAN? The best answer to this question is to contact a competent attorney that you trust to discuss your personal situation and to secure recommendations. Among those who may need a formal estate plan prepared are: (1) individuals with assets of $600,000 or more; (2) business owners; (3) divorced individuals with minor children; (4) handicapped dependents or elderly under your care; (5) those desiring to make special charitable contributions. While this list is not meant to be complete, it does give you some idea of those who may have special estate planning needs. Again, our recommendation is that you do not delay— contact an attorney you trust and discuss your situation and needs. This is one area of your financial plan that you should act upon now—procrastination could prove emotionally and financially disastrous to your loved ones.

WINNING FINANCIAL STRATEGY #10:
IMPLEMENT YOUR PLAN

The hardest part of any plan is its implementation. The purpose of this chapter has been to provide you with some winning financial strategies that will enable to gain control (and keep control) of your personal finances. Your task is to implement those strategies that are applicable to your personal financial situation. Once your plan has been implemented, it should be reviewed in its entirety at least once a year. You will want to involve those members of your financial team that are relevant to your needs and goals. But remember—you are the one that is ultimately responsible and accountable for your actions and decisions. This is one responsibility that cannot be passed off to someone else. You work hard to achieve success in the operation of your store. Work equally hard to achieve success in this important area of your life.

DOCUMENT	WHERE TO KEEP	HOW LONG TO RETAIN
Birth certificate, marriage license, and divorce papers	Safe deposit box	Indefinitely
Military service records	Safe deposit box	Indefinitely
Vehicle titles	Safe deposit box	Until sale or discard
Real estate deeds	Safe deposit box	Until transfer of property
Household inventory	Safe deposit box (with working copy at home)	Keep current
Will	Lawyer and safe deposit box	Indefinitely
Contracts	Lawyer and safe deposit box	As long as current
Home purchase and home improvement records	Home and safe deposit box	As long as you own the home or are rolling over its profits into new homes
Insurance policies	Home (with policy numbers in safe deposit box)	Keep all life insurance policies, but otherwise retain only current policies
Stock or bond certificates	Broker	Until cashed in or sold
Investment purchase and sale records *	Home and broker	Six years after tax filing deadline in year of sale
Tax returns *	Home	Six years from filing date
Cancelled checks and bank statements *	Home	Six years
Receipts for large purchases	Home	Until sale or discard of item
Service contracts and warranties	Home	Until expiration
List of credit cards with account numbers	Home	Keep current

* Generally, the IRS will only audit you three years after filing, but it can go after large underpayments of tax as far back as six years and fraud indefinitely.

Illustration 11.1—Summary of Important Documents

Net Worth Statement

Date: _____

ASSETS (What You Own):

Cash or Liquid Assets
1. Cash and Checking Account(s) $ _____
2. Savings Accounts _____
3. Money Market Funds _____
4. Life Insurance Cash Values _____
5. U.S. Savings Bonds _____
6. Other _____
7. Total Liquid Assets (Add Lines 1-6) $ _____

Marketable Investments (Market Value)
8. Common Stocks $ _____
9. Preferred Stocks _____
10. Bonds (Corporate & Municipal) _____
11. Mutual Funds _____
12. Other _____
13. Total Marketable Investments (Add Lines 8-12) $ _____

Nonmarketable Investments (Current or Estimated Value)
14. Ownership in Business $ _____
15. Vested Company Profit-Sharing or Pension Plan _____
16. Real Estate Investments _____
17. Notes Receivable (Loans to Others) _____
18. Annuities _____
19. IRAs or Keogh _____
20. Total Nonmarketable Assets (Add Lines 14-19) $ _____

Personal Assets (Current Value)
21. Residence $ _____
22. Automobiles _____
23. Furniture _____
24. Equipment _____
25. Jewelry _____
26. Collectibles _____
27. Other _____
28. Total Personal Assets (Add Lines 21-27) $ _____

TOTAL ASSETS (Add Lines 7, 13, 20 and 28) $ _____

LIABILITIES (What You Owe):

Loans (Outstanding Balances)
29. Charge/Credit Card Accounts $ _____
30. Unpaid Bills _____
31. Bank _____
32. Margin _____
33. Insurance _____
34. Installment (e.g., car loan) _____
35. Other _____
36. Total Loans (Add Lines 29-35) $ _____

Mortgages (Outstanding Balances)
37. Personal Residence $ _____
38. Other Real Estate _____
39. Total Mortgages (Add Lines 37 and 38) $ _____

TOTAL LIABILITIES (Add Lines 36 and 39) $ _____

NET WORTH (Total Assets Minus Total Liabilities) $ _____

Illustration 11.2—Sample Net Worth Statement

Estimating What Comes In*

	You	Spouse	Total
Salary, Bonus, etc.	$ _____	$ _____	$ _____
Dividends	_____	_____	_____
Investments	_____	_____	_____
Interest	_____	_____	_____
Savings Account	_____	_____	_____
_____	_____	_____	_____
_____	_____	_____	_____

	You	Spouse	Total	
TOTAL ANNUAL INCOME	$ _____	$ _____	$ _____	Divide By 12
	Estimated Monthly Income		$ _____	

*Estimate numbers for the coming year. Be conservative!

Illustration 11.3A—Budget Worksheet: Income

Estimating What Goes Out

Personal Budget—Monthly   Month _____

1. Estimated monthly income (from preceding page) $ _____

	Planned**	Actual
Fixed Expenditures*		
2. Rent/Mortgage		
3. Utilities		
4. Food		
5. Clothing		
6. Taxes		
7. Social Security		
8. Medical/Dental		
9. Loan Repayments		
10. Auto Maintenance/Repair		
11. Life Insurance Premiums		
12. Other Insurance Premiums		
13. Current School Expenses		
14. _____		
15. _____		
16. Total Fixed Expenditures		
Discretionary Expenditures*		
17. Vacation		
18. Recreation/Entertainment		
19. Charity		
20. Furniture		
21. Investments***		
22. IRA Contributions***		
23. Savings***		
24. _____		
25. _____		
26. Total Discretionary Expenses		
27. Total Expenses (Add Lines 16 and 26)		

Subtract Line 27 from Line 1. If the result is positive, you haven't accounted for all your spending. If the result is negative, you are spending more than you are taking in.

* If you pay any item other than monthly, you must convert the expense to a monthly item. For example, if you pay an expense once a year, divide by 12 to convert to a monthly expense.

** Base your planned expenses on last month's expense. Estimate these using last month's check book and charge account statements. To help monitor expenses, you may want to use checks or credit cards for all expenses over $10.

*** Include what you want to save. That way you can treat this item as an expense and budget for it. Start with 5-10%.

Illustration 11.3B—Budget Worksheet: Expenses

What is our biggest asset?

The biggest asset we have is our ability to get up every day and earn a living. If we can keep doing it we will earn a fortune:

Potential earnings to age 65

Present age	Average income to age 65						
	$25,000	**$35,000**	**$45,000**	**$55,000**	**$65,000**	**$75,000**	**$85,000**
20	1,125,000	1,575,000	2,025,000	2,475,000	2,925,000	3,375,000	3,825,000
25	1,000,000	1,400,000	1,800,000	2,200,000	2,600,000	3,000,000	3,400,000
30	875,000	1,225,000	1,575,000	1,925,000	2,275,000	2,625,000	2,975,000
35	750,000	1,050,000	1,350,000	1,650,000	1,950,000	2,250,000	2,550,000
40	625,000	875,000	1,125,000	1,375,000	1,625,000	1,875,000	2,125,000
45	500,000	700,000	900,000	1,100,000	1,300,000	1,500,000	1,700,000
50	375,000	525,000	675,000	825,000	975,000	1,125,000	1,275,000
55	250,000	350,000	450,000	550,000	650,000	750,000	850,000
60	125,000	175,000	225,000	275,000	325,000	375,000	425,000

When you retire it won't matter how much you earned, what will matter is how much you saved.

Illustration 11.4—How Much Will You Earn During Your Lifetime?

Illustration 11.5A—How Much Life Insurance Will You Need?
HOW MUCH LIFE INSURANCE?

A. ANNUAL FAMILY LIVING COSTS (from Budget form) _____

B. SOURCES OF INCOME AVAILABLE

• Spouse's Income _____

• Social Security Benefits _____

• Income from Income-Producing
Assets (from Budget form) _____

• Income from Proceeds of Existing Life Insurance Policies
(use an assumed rate of interest)

6%—multiply amount of insurance by .06
10%—multiply amount of insurance by .10
12%—multiply amount of insurance by .12

_____ × .10 = _____

• Other Sources of Income _____

TOTAL SOURCES OF INCOME _____

C. ADDITIONAL INCOME NEEDED (subtract B from A) _____

D. AMOUNT OF MONEY TO MAKE UP SHORTAGE
(at an assumed rate of interest)

6%—divide by .06
10%—divide by .10
12%—divide by .12
_____ ÷ .10 _____

E. ADDITIONAL CASH REQUIREMENTS

Final Expenses _____

Education for Children _____

Liabilities (including Mortgage) _____ _____

F. INSURANCE NEEDS (D plus E) _____

Illustration 11.5B—How Much Disability Income Insurance Will You Need?
HOW MUCH DISABILITY INSURANCE?

A. ANNUAL FAMILY EXPENSES _____

B. SOURCES OF INCOME

• Spouse's Net Income _____

• Social Security Benefits _____

• Disability Benefits from Work _____

Income from Income-Producing Assets
(Assets Evaluation form) _____

• Other Income _____

TOTAL SOURCES OF INCOME _____

C. ADDITIONAL ANNUAL INCOME NEEDED
(Subtract B from A) _____

D. MONTHLY BENEFIT NEEDED _____

116

Social Security and Disability

69% of all disability claims are rejected by Social Security

The Social Security Administration rejects 691 disability claims out of every 1,000 it receives. That means seven of every 10 people who apply never collect Social Security benefits for their claim.

The reason for the foregoing is the way disability is defined in the law. For example, only those who are presumed to be disabled for at least 12 months are able to qualify for benefits. There are many other extremely stringent requirements.

Source: Social Security Administration—Office of Operational Policy and Procedures, Office of Disability Program

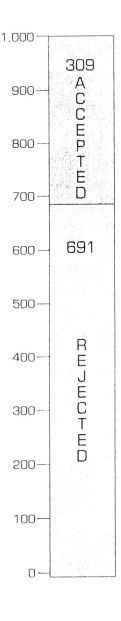

1,000 —	
900 —	309 ACCEPTED
800 —	
700 —	
600 —	691
500 —	
400 —	REJECTED
300 —	
200 —	
100 —	
0 —	

Illustration 11.6—The Reality of Social Security and Qualifying for Disability Income Benefits

DISABILITY UNDER SOCIAL SECURITY

In order to qualify for social security disability benefits an applicant must meet *all* nine of the following tests:

1. He is fully insured by: (1) accumulating 40 quarters of coverage (a total of ten years of covered work); or (2) accumulating at least six quarters of coverage provided he has acquired at least as many quarters of coverage as there are years elapsing after 1950 (or, if later, after the year in which he reaches age 21) and before the year in which he becomes disabled.

2. He has worked under Social Security for at least five of the 10 years (20 out of 40 quarters) just before becoming disabled, or if disability begins before age 31 but after age 23, for at least one-half of the quarters after reaching age 21 and before becoming disabled (but not less than six).

3. He is unable to engage in "any substantial gainful work which exists in the national economy," whether or not such work exists in the area, a specific vacancy exists, or the applicant would be hired if he or she applied for the work (however, consideration is given to age, education, and work experience).

4. Such inability results from "a medically determinable physical or mental impairment" which is expected to result in death, or which has lasted (or can be expected to last) for a continuous period of not less than 12 months. A special definition of the term "disability" is provided for individuals age 55 or over who are blind.

5. He is under 65 years of age.

6. He has filed an application.

7. He has furnished the required proof of disability.

8. He has fulfilled a five month waiting period.

9. He accepts state vocational rehabilitation services or has good cause for refusal.

Illustration 11.7—Nine Qualifying Tests to Receive Social Security Disability Benefits

Illustration 11.8A—Consumer Debt Worksheet

LIST OF DEBTS

Date _____

CREDITOR'S NAME	TYPE OF LOAN	DATE OF LAST PAYMENT	MATURITY DATE	MONTHLY PAYMENT From Budget	TOTAL AMOUNT DUE From Net Worth Statement

TOTAL MONTHLY PAYMENTS $

TOTAL AMOUNT OWED $

Illustration 11.8B—Calculating Your Debt-To-Income Ratio

PERSONAL DEBT RATIO

Your ratio is based on take-home pay. You have figured out the amount of debt that you owe for installment loans. Is this too much for you?

		Monthly	Year
1.	Your total take-home pay	$	
2.	Use 15% (a safe amount for most consumers). Divide income by 6.7 or use 20% (maximum for most consumers). Divide by 5.	$	
3.	Your present installment obligations	$	
4.	Your present safety margin—subtract line 3 from line 2.	$	
5.	Your present ratio—divide your installments obligation (line 3) by your take-home pay (line 1).	$	

It might be wise to use both the 15% and 20% figures to see the difference in your own situation.

119

CHAPTER 12

PERSONAL LEADERSHIP DYNAMICS: MANAGING WITH PURPOSE AND VISION

We know not of the future, and cannot plan for it much. But we can hold our spirits and our bodies so pure and high, we may cherish such thoughts and such ideals, and dream such dreams of lofty purpose, that we can determine and know what manner of men we will be whenever and wherever the hour strikes that calls to noble action. . . . No man becomes suddenly different from his habit and cherished throught.
—Joshua L. Chamberlain, General Commander,
20th Maine, Union Forces, Battle of Gettysburg

INTRODUCTION

So much has been said and written about personal leadership. We look for personal leadership qualities in others. We judge a person's worth and value by their ability to exhibit personal leadership characteristics. We lament the lack of "leadership" in our politicians, presidents, athletes, and executives. We buy books on the subject of leadership by the millions. But what is "leadership" and why is its acquisition so important to so many people? One of the clearest and most challenging definitions of personal leadership I have ever read comes from Paul J. Meyer. In the introduction to his study on The Dynamics of Personal Leadership Mr. Meyer defines personal leadership in this way:

Personal leadership is the self-confident ability to crystallize your thinking so that you are able to establish an exact direction for your own life, to commit yourself to moving in that direction and then to take determined action to acquire, accomplish, or become whatever that goal demands.

The success you achieve in your efforts to build a growing and profitable retail store will in no small part be determined by your ability to lead. To lead yourself and to lead others. This chapter will focus on developing an understanding of the personal qualities that are common to those who would be strong, effective, and successful leaders.

1. EFFECTIVE LEADERSHIP QUALITIES ARE FIRST PERSONAL AND INTERNAL.

As Meyer rightly points out, effective leadership must first of all be personal. Those who would achieve success as leaders must first look deep within themselves to examine and evaluate personal character; to examine and evaluate the very principles that make you who you are. The great mistake so many make is to think that effective leadership qualities can simply be studied, understood, then adopted and applied in one's life. You want to become a better golfer? Read some books on technique, take some lessons from a golf pro, and apply what you have learned. Unfortunately, the same approach when applied to developing effective personal leadership qualities will almost always fail. Why? Because this approach begins with a wrong premise. It begins with the premise that leadership qualities are external to the individual and all that is necessary to become an effective leader is to learn them and then apply them to your own life. But the essence of true leadership can never be separated from the essence of who you are as a person. Personal character and principle are the starting points for understanding the true meaning of effective personal leadership. These qulaities are internal, not external. Simply reading about "the techniques of effective leadrship" and trying to apply those techniques to your own life will not result in you becoming an effective leader. Effective leaders manifest qualities and characteristics that set them apart from others not because they have studied and read from the "experts" on the subject; effective leaders are effective because of their internal, personal qualities and characteristics.

2. EFFECTIVE LEADERSHIP MUST FOCUS ON THE TOTALITY OF LIFE.

Effective leaders are individuals who have come to understand one of life's great principles: no one part of your life can be emphasized without affecting all other areas of your life. You have been created with the ability to think and reason, to love and hate, to work and rest, to achieve and to fail. Your life is made up of a complex of activities that are ongoing and many times overlapping. To consciously focus on developing one activity of your life for a prolonged period of time will inevetably have an adverse effect on all the other areas and activities of your life. For example, suppose you feel out of shape and overweight. So you decide to start exercising regularly and to go on a diet. After a while, your quest to lose weight and to exercise begin to dominate your life. That's all you think about. You so focus on your weight and on exercising that you start to neglect the other areas and activities of your life. The result? A life out of balance. A life in which the pursuit of one worthy activity negatively affects other, equally worthy, activities in your life. Those who would be effective leaders recognize the absolute importance of integrating all activities of life. Effective leaders strive for balance and harmony in the pursuit of every goal, desire, or ambition in life. There are a number of areas, or activities, in life which effective leaders consciously focus on developing and cultivating on a daily basis. They include:

(1) Family Relationships. There can be no greater goal in life than to develop and cultivate strong, loving, and faithful relationships with those you love. Effective leaders are those who recognize the supreme importance of first becoming effective leaders in the home. This type of leadership is rooted in love and a sincere desire to lead by example. It is never dictatorial or intimidating. Effective leaders will focus daily on creating opportunities for strengthening the bonds of family love.

(2) Spiritual Strengthening. Strong, effective leaders recognize the importance of developing and cultivating a strong spiritual life. Your spiritual values reflect all that is ultimately important to you as a person. Seeking spiritual strength is not a mark of weakness, rather it is the true measure of a person's worth and character. Effective leaders are not afraid of what others may say or how they may be viewed in the eyes of the world. True leaders are unwavering in their commitment to the pursuit of the moral and ethical values that make a person, and a society, strong. They serve as an example for their children and for others that come in contact with them.

(3) Physical Development. Effective leaders recognize the importance of taking care of their body as well as their mind and soul. The regular exercise of the body will help promote health, physical strength, and the vigor necessary to live a full and productive life. Effective leaders will set aside time on a regular and consistent basis for this purpose. A strong, healthy body will enable you to work harder, more effeciently and effectively, and for longer periods of time.

(4) Financial Development. Effective leaders will be engaged in the pursuit of noble and worthwhile financial goals. As we stated in chapter 11, achieving true success as a retailer requires that you seize and maintain control of your personal and business finances. This means that you must set your financial goals, establish a workable plan to achieve those goals, and then to implement your plan. In the pursuit of your financial goals, never lose sight of the importance of using your money in a morally and ethically responsible way. One of the marks of true leadership— leadership based on and rooted in strong core principles— is the desire to give as well as receive. It may sound trite, but principled-centered leaders will seek out others with which to share a portion of the material blessings they have been privileged to receive. Again, the key principle is balance. Effective leaders will strive to

achieve balance in developing and implementing any financial program.

(5) Career Development. Effective leaders recognize the importance of the growth-principle. The growth-principle states that any organism will either be in a state of growth and development or in a state of deterioration and regression. Your career should be important to you. Effective leaders will devote time and attention to growing in their abilitiy to become more effective and proficient in their chosen careers. You should be setting time aside to take courses, to attend classes, to read, so that you can continuously be on the cutting edge of your vocation. The pursuit of career excellence should be part of your balanced approach to living your life to the fullest possible extent.

Effective leadership is characterized by a commitment to living a balanced life. Effective leaders will be engaged in the balanced pursuit of developing and cultivating their careers, finances, bodies, families, and their spiritual life.

3. EFFECTIVE LEADERSHIP MUST BE PRINCIPLED-CENTERED.

Perhaps the most profound and valuable book I have read in the last decade on the subject of leadership has been Stephen R. Covey's *Principled-Centered Leadership* (1990, published by Simon & Schuster). Unlike most books on the subject of personal leadership, Covey begins with the premise that "the key to dealing with the challenges that face us today is the recognition of a principled-centered core within both ourselves and our organizations . . ." and that understanding and applying these principles will result in "building personal and professional relationships in order to enjoy a more balanced, more rewarding, more effective life."

Covey makes the insightful observation that effective leaders lead their lives and manage their relationships around a core of unchanging and time-honored principles, while ineffective leaders attempt to manage their time around priorities and their tasks around goals. Leadership effectiveness grows out of a person's inner character and will always reflect that individual's core beliefs and principles. Do you want to become an effective leader? Then look inside a take a measure of those core beliefs and principles that make you who you are. Effective leaders are individuals concerned about character and principle before activities and tasks. Effective leaders become effective not simply because they wake up one day and "resolve to become an effective leader." Resolutions alone will never produce long-term results. Covey points out that we make two mistakes regarding the making of personal resolutions to change certain negative aspects of our lives. First, he states that we do not have a clear knowledge of who we are. And second, we do not have a clear picture of where we want to go in our lives. There are "powerful restraining forces" that make accomplishing resolutions on a long-term basis very difficult in spite of our personal commitment to change bad habits. Those restraining forces include, among other things, (1) appetites and passions; (2) pride and pretension; and (3) aspiration and ambition. Covey states that we can overcome these obstacles by making and keeping three universal resolutions:

First, to overcome the restraining forces of appetites and passions, resolve to exercise self-discipline and self-denial. Effective leaders are characterized as men and women who are in control of their lives. They recognize the importance of leading disciplined and balanced lives. They work very hard at not letting one pursuit (getting in good physical shape or accumulating material wealth and power, for instance) dominate all other areas of their life. These leaders are effective precisely because they exercise daily control over their passions and appetites. Permissiveness, the pursuit of pleasure at any cost, and over-indulgence— while certainly a common characteristic of many in our society— are activities recognized as being the source of much that wrong with those who would be effective leaders today. Resolve to develop and cultivate an inner character marked by self-discipline and self-denial.

Second, to overcome the restraining forces of pride and pretension, resolve to work on character and competence. Socrates said, "The greatest way to live with honor in this world is to be what we pretend to be." Understanding what your core values and principles are is the first step in being able to live in harmony with yourself. Nothing is sadder than to observe someone attempting to be something in public you know they are not in private. This type of hypocrisy can create serious inner struggles and conflicts in the minds and hearts of those individuals who live lives in public that are not consistent with their core values and principles. To become the effective leader you want to be, resolve today to develop the qualities of character and competence.

Third, to overcome the restraining forces of unbridled aspiration and ambition, resolve to dedicate your talents and resources to noble purposes and to provide service to others. Learn to live your life for worthy causes and principles. Eschew the attitude of so many would-be leaders today who "look out for number one" and are more concerned about "what's in it for me" than the welfare and well-being of others. Effective leaders live lives marked by consistency of character and purpose. Their character will shape their purpose in life. This type of leader is sincerely concerned about being a person who not only makes promises and commitments to others, but is equally concerned about being the type of person who will honor their commitments and will keep their promises. Effective leaders are deeply concerned about integrity and honesty in all relationships with others. Resolve today to dedicate your talents and resources to noble and worthwhile purposes and to provide service to others.

These three resolutions should be at the top of your list. You do not need to wait until the new year to make them. Do it today and hold yourself accountable for every action you perform and every word you speak. These are universal resolutions that every effective leader must make and keep. Learn to become a person that can first make and keep self-promises. To break old habits of the past and to develop the inner strength to handle difficult situations in the future, Covey suggests that effective leaders do the following five things:

(1) Never make a promise to yourself or others you will not keep.
(2) Make meaningful promises, resolutions, and commitments to do better and to be better— and share these with a loved one.
(3) Use self-knowledge and be very selective about the promises you make.
(4) Consider every promise as a measure of your integrity and faith in yourself.
(5) Remember that your personal integrity or self-mastery is the basis for your success with others.

4. EFFECTIVE LEADERSHIP IS MARKED BY A COMMITMENT TO INNOVATION.

Anne Morrow Lindbergh once observed that "The wave of the future is coming and there is no fighting it." Effective leaders are consistently thinking not only about what is happening today, they are equally concerned about what will be happening in the future. Effective leaders plan for the future by becoming effective innovators. Denis E. Waitley and Robert B Tucker, in their Book *WINNING THE INNOVATION GAME* (1986, Fleming H. Revell Company), make the following observation about entrepreneurs and innovators: "The entrepreneur finds a need and fills it. The innovator anticipates or creates a need and fills it." Effective leaders in the 90's and beyond will be characterized not only by an ability to inspire and motivate others, they will be characterized by an ability to anticipate future needs and to react before others do to meet those needs. They will not only be strong personal leaders, they will be leaders capable of building successful and profitable businesses. Waitley and Tucker have identified five sources of innovative opportunities most often cited by the innovators they interviewed for their book. Those five sources of innovative opportunity are:

(1) Effective leaders will observe a trend and come up with a way of exploiting it.
(2) Effective leaders will search for solutions to negative trends.
(3) Effective leaders will look at current activities, beliefs, and interests for ideas that might appeal to others.
(4) Effective leaders will come up with a new idea when a present trend is running against them.
(5) Effective leaders will watch what the competition is doing, and do it better.

Strong, effective leaders strive for excellence in every activity of their lives—in their personal and family activities, in their business relationships, and in building successful and profitable businesses. *The pursuit of excellence must first of all be a matter of the mind before it becomes a matter of fact.* We have sought in the writing of this book to provide sound, proven, and practical strategies that will enable you to become, and to remain, successful retailers. The one thing we cannot do is to apply the principles and techniques for you. That is your responsibility. The measure of an effective leader is the ability and the desire to take the initiative to accomplish goals and objectives. We conclude this chapter and our book by repeating Paul J. Meyer's definition of personal leadership:

> *Personal leadership is the self-confident ability to crystallize your thinking so that you are able to establish an exact direction for your own life, to commit yourself to moving in that direction and then to take determined action to acquire, accomplish, or become whatever that goal demands.*

We challenge you to develop the self-confidence necessary to become the kind of leader you desire to be. We challenge you to chart a positive direction for your life, as well as those you love and those you lead. We challenge you to commit yourself to the consistent practice of those deeply held principles, convictions, and beliefs that will set you apart as a principled-centered leader. If you do, you will achieve a degree of success known only to a very few in this life.

GLOSSARY OF TERMS

[Note: The terms and definitions offered here are not intended to be comprehensive nor complete. They are intended to provide a general description of the retail and business terms discussed in this book rather than precise technical definitions.]

Accent Lighting. Special lighting such as track lights, recessed spot lights, or individual pan lights that serve to highlight, or dramatize, specific merchandise or displays in the store.

Accessories. Supplementary merchandise that enhances a point-of-sale display.

Adjacency. The placement of like retail departments together or near each other so as to create a uniform merchandise flow throughout the store.

Ambient Lighting. A general lighting technique utilizing florescent type light fixtures.

Architect. Licensed professional who plans and designs the construction of retail stores, buildings, or other structures.

Attitude. A state of mind or feeling; one's inner disposition.

Awnings. Roof-like structure that serves as a cover or shelter over a storefront or window. May also be used over interior counter and cash wrap areas.

Balance. The harmonious arrangement of products, fixtures, or merchandise in a store so as to create a sense of proportion among all the elements of the store.

Banners. A specially designed piece of cloth used in a retail store setting to advertise or promote merchandise, products, special sales and price reductions.

Billboarding. Merchandising technique that arranges products on a display beginning at the bottom near the aisle, and moves progressively higher toward the back or rear wall of the store.

Blueprint. Plan or drawing prepared by a professional retail store designer or architect that details the complete layout and design of a retail store including the exterior, interior, space plan, fixture plan, lighting plan.

Budget. Itemized summary of estimated income and expenses for a given period of time.

Business Plan. A comprehensive written document that serves as an operating tool to help a business owner to better manage his business and work toward its success.

Business Success Team. A specially selected group of individuals, each with unique talents and skills, that serve to assist a business owner in the successful operation of the business. Examples include attorney, insurance agent, financial planner, professional store designer, merchandiser, real estate professional, or bank trust officer.

Case Stacking. A merchandising technique that utilizes a product's container to display the product. Several containers may be stacked one on top of another with the top containers used to actually display the product.

Cash Flow. Revenue generated from the sale of products or merchandise for a specified period of time.

Color Blocking. Merchandising technique that arranges product vertically from top to bottom, by package or product color, and from left to right on the fixture display.

Conditioned Response. As relates to retailing, a response or reaction by a customer resulting from predetermined subliminal messages created by specific traffic flow and merchandising design techniques.

Contrast. Merchandising technique that emphasizes product differences in color, design, price, or size.

Curb Appeal. Creating a visually attractive exterior image of your store so that it can be easily seen by customers or potential customers passing by.

Customer Space. The walking space created by the loop traffic flow design designated for customer use.

Destination Purchase. A unique, usually higher priced purchase which the customer wants to make, and will travel farther to make. Examples include: cars, air conditioners, power sports equipment and vehicles, TVs.

Display Riser. A specially designed fixture used to raise merchandise off the floor.

Display. Creatively designed exhibit used to show off products or merchandise.

GLOSSARY OF TERMS

Drive Aisle. An aisle that branches off a main customer aisle and attempts to direct customers to other sections or departments deeper in the store.

Dump Bins. Bins, buckets or other receptacles in which small merchandise items are placed (or "dumped") instead of being neatly arranged in rows on display shelves. Most effective when used to display only one product.

Employee Handbook. Comprehensive document that summarizes a company's philosophy, employment practices, procedures, rules, guidelines, and all other information relevant to developing effective employee and employer relations.

Endcap. The end of a gondola fixture. It usually faces an aisle and has greater exposure to customers. Moving merchandise from a shelf on a gondola to an end cap will promote the sale of that merchandise and to promote impulse sales in general.

Estate Planning. Comprehensive approach to accumulating, preserving, and transferring a person's estate.

Feature Display. A special display located at the front of the store and serves as a "show window" to feature special products or displays.

Financial Plan. Comprehensive document that summarizes the goals, needs, and potential solutions to an individual's financial situation.

First Impressions. The impressions and feelings generated when a person first sees your store, your merchandise, and your employees. The retailer's goal is to create positive first impressions throughout the store— from the exterior to the interior.

Fixtures. Specially designed units used to display retail merchandise and products

Focal Point. Merchandising technique that serves to attract a customer's attention to a specific area within the store, usually from a distance. Focal points are effective in corners where two walls join at 90-degree angles. A diagonal wall can then be constructed at a 45-degree angle to the side walls and be utilized as a merchandise focal point display.

Free Standing Fixtures. Fixture designed to stand alone, usually on the retail floor, to display products.

Front Face. Arrangement of products on the front a shelf or fixture so that the products face the customer and conceal the fixture.

Glass Cubes. Display unit comprised of clear, unbreakable glass used for the display of clothing or merchandise.

Gondola. Free standing base with center support and shelves on both sides and ends (called end caps). They are usually 12 to 16 feet long and about 5 feet high. Shelves are usually adjustable and can be replaced with bins, slanting shelves, or pegboard. A common display fixture in many stores.

Graphic Pollution. Unnecessary use of signs, banners, streamers, and other advertising and promotional items throughout the store. Creates a "visually polluted" look in the store.

Grid System. Common customer traffic flow design technique that arranges store fixtures in long rows through which customers must decide to walk in order to shop for merchandise. Can create a sense of confusion and disorder. Does not promote effective impulse customer buying.

Habit. A recurrent, often unconscious pattern of behavior that is acquired through frequent repetition.

Hard Lines. Merchandise or products not designed to be worn on the body. Includes items such as appliances, electronics, sports and recreation equipment, lawn and gardening equipment.

HI-SAM. Acronym for " Have I Sold Additional Merchandise?" Technique used by sales associates to promote add-on sales by customers. Every time a sale is rung up on the register, the sales associate will offer an additional item to the customer for purchase.

Impulse Purchase. An item purchased by a customer while shopping in the store, which the customer did not initially intend to buy.

Independent Retailer. Store or small retailer which is privately owned and is not part of a chain.

Layout. The graphic contribution to an ad or sign.

Leadership. Inner quality of an individual that encourages others to follow.

Line of Credit. Bank agreement allowing a company or business to borrow at any time up to a preapproved specified amount.

Loop System. Customer traffic flow system that creates a customer walk space area separate from the retail selling space. Promotes more frequent opportunities for customer impulse buying.

GLOSSARY OF TERMS

Manhattan Skyline. Refers to merchandise that reaches above the backbone of a gondola. Usually resembles the "Manhattan skyline." Often distracts customers from viewing other products in that same area.

Mannequin. Life-size full or partial representation of the human body used for the purpose of displaying clothing or related products and merchandise. Mannequins are available in a wide variety of sizes, colors, prices, and styles.

Markdown. A reduction in the selling price of an item. A "sale" is a temporary markdown in price; a "clearance" is a permanent markdown.

Merchandising Specialist (Merchandiser). Individual trained in the effective display of retail products and merchandise.

Merchandising. Techniques used to create effective methods to display and sell retail products and merchandise.

Net Worth Statement. Financial statement that reflects an individual's current assets, less current liabilities, which equal "net worth."

Neutral Colors. Colors such as white, tan, gray, or beige that help "neutralize" store decor so merchandise will stand out.

Platforms. A base of wood with a protective or decorative covering, (brick or simple carpet) on which bulky merchandise can be stacked. Can be a very effective display technique for seasonal merchandise such as grills, Christmas trees, gardening supplies, lubricants and oils, aquariums, etc.

Point of Purchase (POP) Displays. Displays located at the spot where customer meets product. Signs located at that point are called "point of purchase" signs.

Point of Sale (POS). Location where customer pays for merchandise.

Profit. Revenue available after all expenses have been paid.

Promotional Displays. Merchandise displays that seek to promote, or advertise, a specific product or product line.

Reserve Fund. Special fund set aside for the payment of unexpected bills and non-monthly expenses. Fund should be liquid and readily available without financial penalty.

Ribboning. Alternative merchandising technique that displays products on shelves beginning at the left, moving to the right in a reverse-S direction until all products have been placed on the fixture.

Risk. The potential for financial loss. Major financial risks— such as death, disability, liability, property, and health— should be insured.

Seasonal. Retailing description of merchandise that has a short selling period. Examples are plants and shrubbery, Christmas trees, winter coats, bathing suits, snowmobiles and watercraft, and giftwrap.

Showcases. Glass enclosed display units usually used to store and display items such as jewelry, watches, and related products.

Sight Lines. Visual paths created that permit customers an unobstructed view of certain products or merchandise.

Sign Machine. Electronic unit that enables you to create professional looking product and price display signs.

Signage. Term used to describe comprehensive approach to the use of all signs throughout a store, including both exterior and interior signs.

Slatwall. Merchandising material comprised of medium density fiberboard with grooved channels either 3", 4", 6", 8", or 12" on center typically used for the display of merchandise accessories. Panels are 4' by 8' on the horizontal.

Sleeve Out. Refers to the hanging of garments on fixtures in such a way that only the side or sleeve of the garment is visible.

Soft Lines. Includes retail merchandise such as apparel, jewelry, cosmetic lines, personal lines (merchandise that generally applies to the human body).

Space Plan. Professionally prepared document or blueprint that details the actual placement and location of all interior items in a retail store. Usually prepared by a professional store designer, the space plan seeks to maximize the use of all available retail space in the most cost-effective manner possible.

Spread to Fill. Merchandising technique that calls for sales associates to arrange available products from adjoining merchandise areas to a shelf that may be temporarily empty. The objective is to create a "full product look" throughout your store.

GLOSSARY OF TERMS

Store Designer/Planner. Individual professionally trained and skilled in the comprehensive layout and design of retail store environments.

Store Walk-through. An exercise in which the owner (or manager) of a retail store "walks through" the exterior and interior areas of the store for the purpose of identifying ways in which sales can be increased, products more effectively displayed, and customer's needs better met.

Success. Predetermined goal of every business owner. Must be individually defined and desired.

Tonnage. Merchandising technique in which one item or product is displayed in large quantities as part of a special promotion or special purchase. Can be either hard line products or soft line products.

Tower Displays. Vertical glass display units that occupy less retail space than larger, more cumbersome, glass showcases.

Traffic Flow. Retail design concept that seeks to enhance customer traffic flow throughout a store. Effective traffic flow will ensure that customers are guided (subconsciously) to specific areas of the store using a predetermined path (called "customer walk-space"). The primary goal is to promote more impulse buying opportunities.

Trend. A shift in the desirability of a product by the general public.

Turnover. Retail term that describes the frequency with which products are sold and replaced from inventory.

Two Finger Rule. Merchandising technique that calls for products to be arranged on a shelf to within two fingers of the top of the next shelf. The objective is to maximize the use of all available retail space in the store.

Valance. A facia panel, usually laminated or painted, used to hold light fixtures around the perimeter of a wall.

Value. Term that describes a customer's perception of what is received from a retailer after making a purchase. Value is often viewed in broader terms than just price. It can include such things as quality customer service, knowledgeable and courteous employees, quantity of items available for purchase, quality of items available for purchase, service after the sale.

Vendor Fixture. Fixture offered to retailer, usually at no cost, for the specific purpose of displaying a vendor's product or merchandise.

Vertical Merchandising. Technique that is used in conjunction with color blocking of products and emphasizes the vertical arrangement of products on a shelf or wall to maximize visibility of the merchandise.

Visibility Curve. Arrangement of merchandise on gondola shelves in such a way that the customer can see the entire display in an unobstructed manner from a standing position while looking at the fixture. Merchandise should be viewed from the top shelf to the bottom shelf without having to lean over.

RDA— READY TO HELP...

Retail Design Associates offers a wide range of professional services to the retailing industry. Whether you are an existing store considering a remodel, upgrade, or new store, or whether you are just considering the possibilities of starting your own retail store, *RDA* can assist you. With a combined total of over forty-five years of retail store and business management experience between them, Jim and Jerry Rasmus stand ready to help you identify existing or potential problems and to develop workable solutions. Our goal: to enable you to increase sales, increase profits, and to enhance your store's image.

RDA offers the following professional store design and management services:

—- Comprehensive Store Walk-through and Analysis

—- Space Design and Utilization Planning

—- Merchandising Seminars and Workshops

—- Decor Analysis and Evaluation

—- Fixture Analysis and Evaluation

—- Fixture Purchasing

—- Comprehensive Interior and Exterior Store Design

—- Signage and Graphics

—- Visual Presentation

—- Customer Service Workshops

—- Financial Planning Consulting

—- Training and Motivational Programs For Employees

At *RDA*, we stand ready to help you develop the winning strategies necessary for continued success in today's competitive retailing marketplace. Give us a call today to discuss your needs and questions.

RETAIL DESIGN ASSOCIATES
7080 Donlon Way
Suite 222B
Dublin, CA 94568
(510) 829-8030 FAX: (510) 829-8032 Or Toll Free: 1-800-722-4922